Never Lose Hope

Peter N Muya

Published by Peter N Muya.

Never Lose Hope

Peter N Muya

Published by BISHOP PETER N MUYA, 2024.

NEVER LOSE HOPE
PETER N. MUYA
First edition. July 2024.
Second edition. June 2025
Copyright © 2025 Peter N Muya.
ISBN 9798224305698

For information contact Bishop Peter Muya via muyabishop@gmail.com
Phone: +254724805868/+254798649468
Edited by Peter Hinga Kiago. Email: quibpet3r@gmail.com
Phone: +254706488565

Table of Contents

DEDICATION

I Joyfully dedicate this book to my brothers, sisters and their children who are ministers of the gospel in different parts of the country.

"Will the world leaders give us solutions to the climate change crisis?"
Bishop Peter N. Muya

Foreword

This inspiring book is a wake-up call for all pastors in our churches in Africa. Bishop Peter has announced his plans to empower the ministers of the gospel to go out to minister hope to the hopeless and the needy in this hurting world. His passion has led him to write this important life- changing book to inspire ministers of the Gospel to do community work.

I consider this to be the most encouraging message of reaching and ministering to the hurting. God gave the author a vision of reaching the unreached and giving hope to the hopeless in Africa. He is asking all ministers to come out of their comfort zones and go out to serve by meeting people's needs. Let us do just like our master Jesus Christ who healed the sick and helped the sinners to repent their sins and be converted.

Question when we look around our communities in Africa what do we see? There are so many refugees, homeless, hopeless, hungry and sick People. War, sickness and famine are the most common emerging issues in the community.

The continent of Africa is walking in total darkness unless we wake up, a rise and shine. millions of hopeless people will perish. Let's be the light of Africa before it's too late. The good news is that we are called by God to reach the unreached and give hope to the hopeless in Africa. Africa belongs to God.

Bishop Kim Kihuguru.

Preface

On that particular morning, I work up as usual with my hangovers and occasional distressing bout of anxiety. I was born in the ghetto in the outskirts of the city of Nakuru and raised in the settlement farm by poverty Stricken Parents.

As a farmer, I endured suffering from famine and drought. I hustled up for food, jobs and burnt charcoal in Kiambogo village to feed my siblings. But this time I could not control myself because the power of the love of God was very heavy in my soul.

I read a book by Billy Graham titled, World Aflame, as I read through it, I cried to God with a loud voice, "Save Me Lord "God's sacrificial love burst in to my troubled soul like a bomb. I confessed my sins and surrendered my miserable life to Jesus Christ. I was born again and transformed. Gods sacrificial love was manifested in my life. "God shows his love towards us, that while we were yet sinners Christ died for us" (Romans 5-8)

I was wallowing in sin and suffering without knowing that the full price had already been paid for my salvation. I started witnessing in the village and I became an evangelist. Nobody expected that I could succeed, but eventually, I became a pastor and a patron of a community based organization.

Knowing what it means to be hungry and malnourished, I volunteered to be a messenger of hope to millions of Kenyan families who were at a high risk of food insecurity and malnutrition.

Never Lose Hope, is a true story of how people in this hurting world can be helped to overcome the fear of the unknown and navigate through life by trusting the creator of all things. Modern science technology and our increased knowledge have failed to give us hope for survival.

I believe that this book is written to encourage you not to never lose hope. In my Christian life I have learnt to trust God in all situations, I have endured hardship, afflictions, and hard situations which have been bringing me to my knees, so to speak. God gave me a thrilling visitation of giving hope to the hopeless in this hurting world.

When I remember what God has done in my life, I am encouraged to lead others to experience God's sacrificial love. "It is of the Lords Mercy that we are not consumed, because his compassion fails not" (Lamentation 3-21-22). The steadfast love of God never ceases, his Mercies never come to an end, and they are new every morning, great is his faithfulness.

Read this book and you will discover the secret of survival and experience Gods sacrificial love in your trouble life. With God everything is possible. "Never lose Hope"

Read this book and your miserable life will be transformed. Through Gods redemptive love my life was changed, from a hustler to a Bishop. God is faithful.

Acknowledgement

I would want to thank Mr. Mburu who did the type setting of this manuscript and my editor Peter Hinga for the good work.

Chapter 1

A CHRISTMAS WITH A DIFFERENCE.

My soul; was crying for freedom, but I did not know that Christmas means salvation from sins and all evils. I was living in sin, in pleasure, and in the desires of the body without knowing that the price for my salvation was paid in full. God paid the price, and Jesus was the reason for the season.

I was yearning for a Christmas with a difference. *I wanted a Christmas with meaning; a Christmas that would last forever. A Christmas that is fulfilling, despite my circumstances.* I wanted to cry to God and believe His wonderful promises. I wanted to be set free.

The word of God came to me, and I started to meditate upon the scripture, "A child is born for us and He is a wonderful counselor, mighty God, Everlasting Father, the Prince of Peace" (Isa. 9:6).

On that particular morning, I woke up as usual with my hangovers and occasional distressing bouts of anxiety. But this time, I could not control myself because the power of the love of God was very heavy in my soul. I read a book by Billy Graham titled *World Aflame*. As I read through it, I cried to God with a loud voice, "Save me, Lord!" Suddenly, God's power burst into my troubled soul like a bomb.

I mourned bitterly for my soul in the presence of God as I confessed all of my sins and invited Jesus Christ into my heart. I was saved and forgiven. I was set free as I then felt the instant assurance of peace and joy in my soul. I found greater fulfillment in my new life. This was the fulfillment of the prophecy in my life that a child was born in my soul. Praise the Lord! To me, I learned then the real meaning of Christmas. Christmas means salvation.

It is regrettable to note that much attention during Christmas is paid to what they call the Christmas tree. The tree decorated with tinsel, ornaments, and colored lights, while the rugged tree of the cross where Jesus hung on Calvary is forgotten during the season. Many people work very hard to save a lot of money, which could be used during the season for good purposes. But instead, the money is used for drinking, having sex, and all kinds of pleasures in this evil-filled world. They overlook the real meaning of Christmas.

Jesus was born for only one purpose: saving sinners from their sins. But every year, the true significance of His birth is lost in the decorations, gift-giving, festivals, and parties that are associated with evil and sinful celebrations during this season. Remember that homosexuals and lesbians also celebrate and enjoy this season.

You must all keep in mind that the Son of Man was born in Bethlehem's stable and grew up to become a sacrifice for our sins by hanging on a tree, a savage instrument of execution. As you and I remember our Savior's birth during the season of Christmas, let's be deeply conscious that it is vitally related to Golgotha, the place where Jesus Christ was crucified and shed His blood for the sins of the whole world.

Let us, therefore, not forget the tree of Calvary's cross during the season of Christmas. The tree of Calvary should be an essential part of this season. In this joyous season of the year, we should recall that Jesus was born and died on the tree to provide eternal life to us all. Jesus is the reason for the season of Christmas.

Now, when I wake up in the morning to find that it's Christmas Eve, I try to draw my attention to my savior, Jesus Christ, like John the Baptist. My mission is to direct sinners to the Messiah. I am a gospel messenger of hope. I make sure that all that I do is to drive the hopeless, the lost, the poor, the needy, the oppressed, and the less fortunate to the Redeemer.

I make sure the greeting cards I send to my loved ones, as well as the presents, are motivating people to know the love of God in Jesus Christ, the Messiah. Jesus is the greatest gift that God has given us. Remember. The gift was wrapped with swaddling clothes in a manger in Bethlehem.

I have found that during the season of Christmas in the rural area in Kiambogo village, Elementaita division, Gilgil sub county, Nakuru county. where I come from, you can hear Christians shouting with joyful celebration, "Merry Christmas!"

As they sing African chorales in the churches, you can also hear the beating of drums coupled with original compositions of praise and worship. In the villages everywhere, you can meet cheerful people at night during Christmas Eve announcing the triumphant birth of the King of Kings.

But yet, many rural folks do not know the real meaning of Christmas. Some of these folks fail to understand the reason for this noise of praising, worshipping, dancing, and shouts of "Merry Christmas!" Although they enjoy dancing, they don't understand what it is all about. They can see Christians shouting to the top of their voices that it is Christmas. Many folks are troubled when they see the decorations with the usual religious services in the village during the season.

Many do not welcome the season because they are suffering from famine, floods, earthquakes, civil wars, clashes, and conflicts. Many people have social, physical, and economic crises in their lives, and so, they cannot understand the reason for these celebrations during the season.

Just imagine people spending millions of dollars on gifts, decorations, festivals, and parties while there are millions of hopeless people dying from a lack of food—desperate people without friends with whom to celebrate and dance with. This only deepens their feelings of sorrow and hopelessness. Many people have many different problems, and so, they cannot enjoy the season.

We are messengers of hope to give hope to the hopeless, so let's do something to help the needy during this season. Instead of wasting much money with pleasures for only one season, let us give, and we shall receive the greatest reward in heaven. It is during this season in which we must show that Jesus is alive through practical love. This a chosen time of the year to show the world the true meaning of Christmas by giving to the needy and less fortunate.

It's the time when we are to reach out in love by sharing our resources with the needy: orphans, widows, street children, the destitute, the hopeless, and the less fortunate in life. We can also help them by explaining the gospel and sharing the most magnificent gift with them: the one which God gave to us all. These kinds of acts can help the needy join us in celebrating the day when Jesus was born!

Remember that no matter how much energy you put in celebrating Christmas, you will still be disappointed in your life, and you could even be feeling empty in your soul if you haven't received Jesus Christ in your soul. It is true that your traditional activities, although your friends and relatives could surround you, could all be pointless unless you accept Christ into your soul.

Without Jesus Christ in your soul during the season, you could be celebrating with a feeling that something is missing in your life. Everything could be looking wonderful, but after taking a closer look into your soul, you may realize that without Jesus, your celebration has no meaning.

Remember that it is during this season when the angel of the Lord suddenly appeared in the world with good news for all people, saying, "Do not be afraid, for behold I bring to you good tidings of great joy which shall be for all people" (Luke 2:10).

To us Christians, this is a wonderful season in our lives. We accept it because it is the time when great light and peace came into the whole world. That's why we sing praises as we worship our beloved Savior. "In Him, we have redemption through His own blood and the forgiveness of sins, according to His riches of His grace" (Eph. 1:7).

Jesus is alive in our souls. That's why we do have a wonderful time of anticipation and excitement as we enjoy His peace, joy, and salvation at all times. Our joy is not found only during this season, however; we have joy in our souls every day. These are the glad tidings of great joy to the redeemed. This is the time when even the hosts of heaven join us in joyful celebrations because our Savior is alive. We are called after Him. We are His own.

I know Jesus Christ, my Savior, personally, and so, I will never be moved by empty religious celebrations. Some people regard Christmas as the highest social event of the year in the whole world. During Christmas, we should be experiencing the greatest inner joy and lasting peace in our souls. I shall never take Christmas as the only celebration of fundamental religious significance in my life. Jesus is alive, and He lives in my soul all days of the year. After committing my life to Jesus, I joined the church, and later I joined the ministry. I am a full-time pastor in the Gospel Messengers Church in the city of Nakuru, Kenya.

The messages I preach are very clear: "Behold, a virgin gave birth to a son and they shall call His name 'Emmanuel' - (God with us). The word was fulfilled which says, 'And you shall call His name Jesus, for He will save His people from their sins'" (Matt. 1:21, 23).

The question is, "Are you saved?" If not, why then do you not accept Jesus Christ as your personal savior in your soul now so you will see the difference? You will realize the real meaning of Christmas in your soul. Emmanuel (God with us).

God will be with you in all seasons, and your soul will never be spiritually bankrupt. To some, Christmas is the holiest day in their lives. But to all those who reject Christ, Christmas can be a stumbling block. Many still do not know the true meaning of Christmas.

Let us accept the offer that God has given us, Jesus Christ, and say, "Thank you, Lord!" I'm writing this article to help you realize the true meaning of Christmas because I know many people around the world do celebrate Christmas blindly without knowing the true meaning of it. It is very hard to get the lasting joy and peace that was brought during the Christmas season without receiving Jesus Christ in your soul. When Gods sacrificial love arrested me, I confessed my sins and surrendered my miserable life to Jesus. I was born again and transformed.

Remember that the angel called it, "Glad tidings of great Joy to all people." That's the true meaning of Christmas. Have you received this glad tiding of great joy in your soul? Don't work for your own joy by decorating your own home. You could be celebrating by attending festivals, parties, or exchanges of gifts with your loved ones, but remember that after these man-made excitements, your joy will subside, and you will feel just as empty as before.

What is the use? You will still feel frustrated and empty in your soul because you don't have the source of true and lasting joy, Jesus Christ. This is good news to you personally about Gods sacrificial love. to mankind. God shows His love for us in that, while we were sinners, Christ died for us. Romans.5.8. I Thank God that Jesus saved me!

Chapter 2

NEVER LOSE HOPE.

Modern science – technology and our increased knowledge – has failed to give us hope for survival. It does not matter which technology we subscribe to. Our knowledge is aimed at destroying our own lives. "Who will survive?" people are asking. Millions of people are perishing every day without knowing where to get help. That's why I purposely want to answer the many questions which are being asked by troubled people.

I know you will be encouraged by my living testimony. In the year 1985 God gave me a thrilling vision of reaching the unreached and giving hope to the hopeless in this hurting world. Before I was saved, I was a village farmer who endured suffering from famine and drought because of climate change.

I hustled up for food, jobs and burnt charcoal to feed my siblings. But when Gods love arrested me, I was transformed from a hustler to a gospel messenger. Knowing what it means to be hungry and malnourished, I volunteered to be a messenger of hope to millions of Kenyans who were at a high risk of food insecurity and malnourished. I helped many hurting people to overcome the fear of the unknown. Nobody in the village thought that I could succeed, but eventually, I became an evangelist and later I became a pastor.

As a bishop now, I have a wake-up call to the servants of God to kindly meet the needs of the homeless, the hopeless, the naked, and the hungry in their communities. I have done seminars to revive and renew the spirits of gospel ministers and challenged them to continue with this rewarding ministry. My mission is to help troubled people in order to answer the question, "Who will survive?" You can overcome the fear of the unknown by trusting in the God I know.

In my Christian life I have learnt to trust in God in all situations. I have learnt how to endure hardship, afflictions, and hard situations, which have been bringing me to my knees, so to speak.

I have learnt to be strong through the Lord even in my sixties. I have endured many hard knocks in my life and in the ministry. Sometimes God brings my heart low through tough situations, for He would want to bring me closer to Him than I was before.

Through many hardships and tribulations, I came to a true, deep, and unsophisticated state of genuine submission. God's correction does not bring pleasure to my flesh, but rather it yields the peaceable fruit of righteousness onto those who are exercised thereby. Hebrews 12:11: "With anguish of soul, I cried out as a servant of God, in my afflictions. I knew I am dust and the Spirit of God dwells in me."

> Proverbs 12:1: "Whoever loves discipline loves knowledge, but he who hates reproof is stupid." He who is willing to be disciplined will become wise, while he who refuses to be disciplined will remain a fool. I truly appreciate the trials of my faith that God allows in my life. When I consider where I had been before trials, my heart overflows with gratitude to God for helping me to overcome trials. That is because trials make me better and not bitter, just as a small child takes delight in his or her parents after a rod of correction. I must take delight

in God for His correction rod in my life. Correction proves that I am a genuine child of God and not an illegitimate child.... Read Hebrews 12.5.11.

Since the day the Lord called me into the ministry, I have been struggling to preach the gospel without knowing the full will of God for my life. Therefore, my life had become a battlefield. Even though many people responded positively to my preaching, I had been struggling in my soul without peace of mind. I worked hard for God but without knowing that without a vision in the ministry, I was going to perish. "Where there is no vision, the people perish" (Prov. 29:18).

Surely Africa is vulnerable to many dangerous calamities from diseases, famines, earthquakes, civil wars, and conflicts. Millions of people are suffering and crying in great pain. Others are dying without hope. That's why my ministry's vision is: "Reaching Out for Jesus." I can say, like the apostle, Paul, "I was not disobedient unto the heavenly vision" (Acts 26:19).

The voice of God in my soul has an irresistible divine force in it. I developed a burning passion for souls. I preached the wholesome word of God with power as it fell to sinners with intensifying conviction. I saw sinners weeping openly after an altar call. They confessed their sins, and they received Christ as their personal savior. The glory and the presence of God were manifested in their lives.

I utilized every available means and every opportunity to fulfill my vision. My vision was birthed in prayer, and it is sustained by faith and sparked by the Holy Spirit. My vision is deeply rooted in God. I will make sure that all the nations of Africa will catch the vision. Africa is in my heart, and other nations of the world are in my mind.

I can only echo the cry, "Africa for Jesus." Let it be your cry, too. Uphold Africa in your prayers because what we have done through God's grace is but a drop in the ocean. More souls in Africa need to reach before it is too late. I know my vision will cost me a lot! But despite this, I am ready to be opposed, ridiculed, mocked, beaten, or taken to the police for preaching the gospel.

I will joyfully pay the price for my vision, no matter the cost. I thank God for giving me Joseph's courage, which makes me press on no matter what. God has chosen me, an ordinary person, to make me extraordinary in His kingdom. What an overwhelming experience in my life.

Prophetic confirmation of the vision

IN APRIL OF 1999, WHEN Dr. Morris Cerullo visited Nairobi, Kenya, he spoke a prophetic utterance to the body of Christ in Africa. Cerullo said, "God is going to raise Africans. They will not reach Africa only, but the whole world. I prophesy that every country in Africa will be opened to the gospel! I believe that Africa is going to have the greatest harvest and the greatest manifestation of the power of God that the world has ever seen."

This prophecy was timely because it confirmed my vision and said what God is going to do in Africa. The Bible says, "The prophet which prophesied of peace, when the word of the prophet shall come to pass, then shall the prophet be known that the Lord hath truly sent him" (Jer. 28:9).

My call is to bring Africa to a new purpose and destiny. God has given me a long-term vision, and I will concentrate on it. It has made me remain original and not copy any minister in the ministry. I will prayerfully listen for directions from my God. My sole desire is to please God and not man. I will always preach the undistorted word of God to impart life to many souls in Africa. Through prayers, I will persistently and consistently track my heavenly vision. My prayer is, "Use me, Lord!"

I'm embarking on a quest to reach all of Africa for Jesus because I have seen that millions of people in many nations of Africa are perishing due to famines, civil wars, turmoil, and diseases, while additionally others are crying for deliverance from the increasing HIV/AIDS pandemics.

It is a fact that Africa is shaped like a question mark, but Jesus is the answer for Africa. He knows about every problem in our lives, and He has every solution for all real issues in Africa. Because Jesus is alive, we are going to survive. We can say that although we are troubled on every side, we are not destroyed because Jesus is living in our souls.

Although Africa is on the crossroads of destiny, God is our refuge in every storm. Our help comes from the throne of the king of kings, whose name is El-Shaddai, the All-Sufficient One. Jesus knows all crises in Africa. He was once on a crossroads surrounded by the murderous soldiers, with no escape route from death. All people, even one of His disciples, denied Him.

Despite this, He patiently endured the cross and conquered all things, including death. That's why we are preaching Christ, for we are called to keep reflecting the life of Christ to these bleeding souls in Africa. I am making sure that everybody will receive the light of the gospel. I'm acting on the promises of God. They have built me up and strengthened and encouraged me.

Let us begin mission operations at home, for charity begins at home. I love Africa, and I believe it will be free from sin, oppression, suffering, pain, tears, turmoil, famines, wars, anguish, and financial burdens. Africa needs breakthroughs and visitations. This vision has made my ministry expand and increase from a tiny handful of believers in my village to many believers in the whole country.

We are growing up spiritually. We can boldly resist all the powers of the Devil and opposition coming from both within and outside the ministry. I have a divine certainty and approval that God has called me to serve Him; I have a life-saving mission in Africa. Africa is thirsting for the manifestation of the power of God. God is willing to satisfy and quench our thirsty souls. That is why I am calling, "Africa, awake. Rise and shine, for your light has come."

Peace is scarce in the world today. The media relentlessly confronts us with stories of civil wars, famine, floods, earthquakes, bombings, disasters, calamities, tragedies, sexual harassment, child abuse, HIV/AIDS epidemic, and economic uncertainty.

Many people in Africa are living in harsh and challenging conditions. Some have no strength to press on to live. They are unable to bear the suffering and pain anymore. They are at the point of losing hope for life as they wallow in despair. Every day they are counting their increases in problems, suffering, failures, pains, and losses.

Every day the devil is directing their minds into more trouble. But no matter the complexity of the issues they are battling, we are ministering life and new hope into their hopeless lives. The devil schemes to engage them in battle and push them until they are at the point of being at their wit's end. The devil wants to kill or destroy their lives in many ways.

However, there is hope for all those people in Africa who are suffering from diseases, famines, civil wars, tribal clashes, and other crises. We are given power and authority in the name of Jesus Christ to challenge the devil and push him away. "Say to those who are fearful in heart, 'Be strong, do not fear! Here is your God.'" (Isa. 35:4).

Human beings cause most of the greatest tragedies and crises. They are used by the devil to cause troubles that are beyond our control, making life in Africa uncomfortable and unbearable. Note that some of our sufferings, problems, difficulties, and pains come to us from human sources. They are caused by somebody's sins, failure, ignorance, carelessness, selfishness, or lust for power.

The devil's plans at first seem to have sweetness in them, but they ultimately end up causing wounds, troubles, problems, suffering, pains, and death. Many people today are living with much bitterness due to evil things that had been done to them by somebody in their lives.

Many people in Africa are crying, and some are dying. Their question is: "How long must I bear pain in my soul, and have sorrow in my heart all day? How long shall my enemy be exalted over me?" (Ps.13:2). How long will millions of innocent lives be victimized by these fatal HIV/AIDS epidemic? How long will sorrow and pain rule over lives because of civil wars and famine? How long will we suffer as the casualties of mad gangs who rain terror at will? How long must death rule millions of lives in Africa?

We are now wrestling with our thoughts as pain and sorrow rule our hearts. This is the cry of Africa. That's why we decided to form a community-based organization (CBO) to minister humanitarian aid and minister hope to the suffering, hungry, poor, needy, and destitute, as well as orphans, widows, street children, refugees, and the oppressed. Our CBO is called; Stay Up rehabilitate Community Based Organization. Our mission is to minister hope to the hopeless in Africa. We support and encourage the suffering, poor, and needy. We are working through an international network in our ministry.

The network aims to assist us in reaching the lost, the poor, and the needy in any part of Africa. We are willing to help them in any way possible, be it through prayer or a sharing of resources. We are working with the faithful leaders, ministers, Christian workers, volunteers, and coordinators who help form this network. We are willing to work with other churches, ministries, non-governmental organizations (NGOs), denominations, sponsors, partners' financial supporters, and donors.

We are willing to support and serve others in whatever capacity we might be able to. We have created a channel for sharing resources, information, and ideas in our office in Nairobi. Are you willing to serve the Lord in any of these ways? Do let us know. You can help us launch an effective ministry in this hurting world. The body of Christ in Africa is uniting together by forming this network. This network is very crucial because it is going to function as a central nervous system in the body of Christ in Africa. "Behold, how good and pleasant it is when brothers dwell in unity! For there the Lord has commanded the blessing and forever" (Ps. 133: 1,3).

Together, we are echoing the cry, "Africa for Jesus." Let it be your call, too. What we have done in Africa is but a drop in the ocean. More souls need to be reached before it is too late. Uphold Africa in your prayers. Although peace is indeed rare in our hate-filled, violent Africa, we are declaring peace in troubled Africa in the name of Jesus. Your prayer may be, "The Lord turn His face toward (Africa) and give (Africa) peace" (Num. 6:26). God's peace brings hope, and we are messengers of hope.

Chapter 3

GOD IS DOING A NEW THING IN AFRICA

Where shall we get answers to our questions in Africa? Whether we admit it or not, deep in our souls, there is a craving and thirst for meaning in this life. The many things which we are using to try to quench our thirst seem endless. Trying alcohol and drug abuse leads us to more pain because of the HIV/AIDS epidemics.

Crime leads us to more troubles, such as ending up in jails for years. Conflicts and civil wars lead us to the loss of our loved ones. We are living in a thirsty society, yet we have nothing to satisfy our thirst for meaning. Despite the fact that Africa is suffering in a crossroads dying of great thirst, God has invited us into this presence. "Therefore, with joy shall ye draw water out of the wells of salvation" (Isa. 12:3).

Let's joyfully drink the waters from the wells of life, for in them, we shall have our blessings in Africa. We shall receive our salvation, healing, joy, peace, deliverance, success, and prosperity. God has revealed to us the way to live, for, in His presence, there is fullness life, and in his right hand, there are pleasures forevermore. God is filling the craving in our souls, and we have new hope for a better life, for we have been given access to all the blessings of God.

Many people are waiting to see Africa die. I am a messenger of hope and declare, "I shall not die, but live, and declare the works of the Lord" (Psalms 118:17). I have good news for you. I declare that even you will not die. You will live to preach the gospel to those around you. "Believe in the Lord, your God, so you will be established. Believe His prophets, and you will succeed" (2 Chronicles 20:20).

Africa will not die. Many people have lost hope for Africa, but I declare that Africa will live. Africa belongs to Jesus. God is doing a new thing in Africa. "Remember not the former things; do not consider the things of old. Behold, I am doing a new thing; now it springs forth. Do you not perceive it? I will make a way in the wilderness and in rivers in the desert. The wild beasts will honor me, the jackals and the ostriches, for I give water in the wilderness, and rivers in the desert, to give to my chosen people, the people whom I formed for myself so that they might declare my praise" (Isa. 43:18, 21).

God is doing something new in Africa! It is God who has done great things, miracles, and wonders in the past years. But, He tells us, "Behold, I will do a new thing; now it shall spring forth; shall ye not know it? I will even make a way in the wilderness, [and] rivers in the desert" (Isa. 43:19). In Africa, we are expecting the greatest outpouring of the Holy Spirit through the body of Christ. We are expecting a great spiritual awakening; a revival in our lives. We are expecting the greatest harvest of souls in Africa. "There is pure life in the water of life, clear as crystal, proceeding out of the throne of God and of the Lamb" (Rev. 22:1).

When this river flows and the chosen people of God drink from it, they receive new joy, peace, love, righteousness, and holiness. They are revived; they become so new, exciting, and wonderful since God removes all obstacles in their lives and nothing stands in their way. They receive breakthrough, and this is a new thing.

They have hope; the spirit of the Lord God is within them. They are anointed to preach the good news to the afflicted and the brokenhearted, as well as liberty to the captives. Instead of mourning with a heavy spirit, they receive the oil of joy and begin to praise God, for they are the chosen people; the chosen generation of priests and ministers of God. Instead of becoming ashamed in this world, they eat the wealth of the nations. They receive their double portion, and they are victoriously made full of everlasting joy. Praise and worship fill the house of God with the glory of God. When the river flows through the sanctuary, the house of God becomes a saving, a healing, a deliverance, and a filling station.

The hopeless will come in to receive hope. The sick will come in to receive their healing. The sinners will come to receive their salvation. The captives will come to receive their liberty. The oppressed will come for their deliverance. The discouraged will come for their encouragement. The brokenhearted will come for their restoration. The weak will come for revival. And the dead will come for their resurrection. Amid the confusion, suffering, pain, and despair, the river of life will be moving, and a great multitude will be saved while others will be healed. Everybody is going to have hope again as the flood sweeps in over us, bringing life to any repentant sinner.

God is doing a new thing in Africa! Even though we are living in a hard and challenging time, we are encountering changes everywhere in Africa. We have hope because as the river flows, God meets our needs. He blesses our jobs. Our businesses are healed. Diseases such as HIV/AIDS are being healed everywhere. The river is continually flowing.

The Bible compares the sinners to the jackals and the ostriches. So, sinners are invited to drive this river into the desert or wilderness. It also calls us Christians the chosen people of God, and we are invited to drink from this river so that we can praise God. I can call the Christians "trees of righteousness planted by the Lord so that He might be glorified" (Isa. 61:3).

Jeremiah says, "Blessed is the man who trusts in the Lord, whose trust is the Lord. He is like a tree planted by the water that sends out roots by the stream and does not fear when heat comes, for its leaves remain green; and it is not anxious in the year of drought, for it does not cease to bear fruit" (Jer. 17:7–8).

Job was a minister of hope, like me, for he said, "For there is hope for a tree if it is cut down that it will sprout again, and that the tender branch thereof will not cease" (Job. 14:7). Job had many trials. He was suffering in great pain. He sat in the ashes of his life, family, possessions, health, and marriage, which all looked dead. He was suffering emotionally, spiritually, and physically. However, he was strong in faith. His trust and hope rested on the living God alone. He did not lose hope. "Now faith is the substance of things hoped for, the evidence of things not seen" (Heb. 11:1).

Because of his faith and hope for the things that are not seen, Job refused to die. New shoots were beginning to sprout from the lifelessness of his life. He said, "At least there is hope for a tree. If it is cut down, it will sprout again, and its new shoots will not fail" (Job 14:7). Job likened his life to a tree. He had surely been cut down and was suffering great pain. People, including his wife and friends, told Job to die. Like Job, I have been in such troubling circumstances, but I pause and look at the situation of Job and say, "There is hope for me, because there is hope for a tree that was cut and died, but it sprouted a new shoot.

NEVER LOSE HOPE

Even Jesus Christ was like a tree that had been cut down, but He sprouted; He resurrected with a new life. Jesus's resurrection brings new life into the lifelessness of our sins. "Though its roots have grown old in the earth and its stump decays, at the scent of water it will bud and sprout again like a new seedling" (Job 14:8). The tree had been cut down and its roots had waxed old into the earth. Yet, God was saying that there was hope for this tree.

I love to believe the promises of God so that I can live in faith and hope for the blessings of God. I have experienced the forces of darkness that fight with me, but I have fought back so that I may live in my hope. Hope is a powerful force. Because of hope, I receive the things I hadn't seen yet. Every blessing or breakthrough comes to me by faith and hope. Although I was born into a poverty-stricken family, I have received great success in life because of great expectations and hope. I have hope for a bright and prosperous future.

Hope always raises my heart, no matter what is happening in my life at the moment. If you have hope, it does not matter what people say or think. Your past failures no longer matter. With hope, you will always succeed and never fail. "Yet at the scent of water, it will bud and put forth branches like a young plant" (Job. 14:9).

Abraham and all his descendants lived in hope, and they received their promises. As Christians, because we are likened with a tree, we choose whether we are going to be like a desert shrub or a luxuriant tree. "Blessed [is] the man that walked not in the counsel of the ungodly, nor stranded in the way of sinners, nor sitieth in the seat of the scornful, but rather his delight is in the law the Lord and in His law doth he meditates day and night. And he shall be like a tree planted by the rivers of water, that brought forth his fruit in his season, his leaf also to shake and not wither; and whatsoever he doeth shall prosper" (Ps. 1:1–3).

Any tree that will not remain in the water will die during the dry season. Trees that survive are those whose roots remain deep in the water. Those are Christians who resolutely and consistently trust in God. If you are a Christian who chooses to feed the mind with evil TV programs, videos, or books, or adopt worldly standards and follow the counsel of the ungodly, you will remain very weak spiritually and will be fruitless.

We are called to read, study, and meditate on God's word. We are called to spend time in fellowship with Christ in prayer. Also, we are to fellowship with other Christians. We follow the advice of our pastors so that we may grow strong and become productive and effective in the ministry. Fellowship with Christ is always promoted in the ministry. That's how you can be a tree that is deeply rooted in the waters.

The devil cannot cut you down if you are in close fellowship with Christ. You will live a victorious life full of hope. The devil will not be able to tear you down. You will always be like a tree that is fruitful because of the scent of water, which is the word of God. The word of God is the spiritual avenue for generating hope in your life. Choose to remain deeply in the word, and you will be fruitful in all seasons.

We have been ministering hope to the victims of HIV/AIDS who have been just waiting to die. We read to them the word, that says, "I shall not die, but live, and declare the works of the Lord." Suddenly hope is born in their hearts, and they become ready to receive their healing.

Although they walk and work as usual, the word of God brings hope to the hopeless. Let me assure you that no matter what problem, pain, suffering, or trouble the devil may have brought into your life, believe the word of God, and your hope will rise to receive your miracle from God. You cannot receive a miracle that you have not hoped for. I declare to you that the word of God gives hope, and everything that may be dying in you will become alive again in Jesus's name.

Chapter 4

FROM A HUSTLER TO A BISHOP.

I was born and brought up in a poverty-stricken family. In our family, we were four brothers and five sisters. We lived in a small village in a very humble environment, financially, socially, and morally.

My father was a reckless alcoholic. He would sell some of the few possessions that we had to buy a bottle of "chang'aa." We never enjoyed such things as running water or indoor toilets. My father used all of our money for his alcohol addiction. We had no money to buy a plot of our own. Father was the cause of endless domestic violence at home. Many are the times that he chased us, together with our mum, out of the house and made us sleep outside in the cold night.

Father heaped many physical and emotional waves of abuse on us, but especially on me in particular. Everybody, even the relatives, knew everything that was happening in our lives, but they could do nothing to help us. Many times, he would take his wrath out on me and had made me hate life. I thought that I was useless.

One of the sad facts of life in our family was the evident decay of my father's parental love. He failed in his life because he could not administer fatherly discipline and correction at home, though we had great respect towards him. We were fearful because of the rise of evil activities and crimes displayed by the villagers. Without proper guidance from Father, there was no reason why we should not have also engaged ourselves in evil ways in order to survive in life.

Tragically, my father was the leading cause of all of our problems in the whole family. He was very reckless in life and very loose in his morals. So, as we had no choice, we involved ourselves in all sorts of evils and crimes in the village. Although we didn't realize it at the time, the word of God was relevant: "Woe unto them that call evil good, and good for evil, that put darkness for light, and light for darkness; that put bitter for sweet and sweet for bitter" (Isa. 5:20).

Our family had a threatening tide of lawlessness that was destroying our lives. My father was a commander of nine children and one mother, but he was not aware of the problems in his camp. I was painfully aware of all of the issues and failures within our family in every point of life. I suffered and developed high blood pressure. I carried all the problems of our family in my heart. My heart was unable to bear all of these problems, so I lost control over my fate.

I was utterly unable to cope with the terrible and threatening situations in our home. This caused me and my brother to become involved with fighting in the village. I had two fractures in my right hand, and my brother had two fractures: one in his right leg and the other in his left foot. At one point, both of his legs were covered with a cast for three months.

My brother and I were both drunkards and drug addicts. My sisters became pregnant as soon as they reached puberty, adding more unwanted children and more problems to the family. We were all causing harm in our home and in the village. We were never subject to parental discipline at home, so we joined a gang of criminals in the village.

We were members of a disrupted family brought up in a disrupted society in a disrupted world. My brother and I would assault the villagers as well as the family members at home. Some of our younger sisters and brothers left home to seek safety from this never-ending conflict at home. They went to stay with our relatives. My elder sister engaged herself in prostitution to survive. She died of HIV/AIDS. After two years, my brother died of the same thing. The whole family seemed to be succumbing to alcohol, crime, and drugs, with equal harm to both the family and the community.

Oh what a miserable life; A life without meaning or purpose. My life was horrible because, I was brought up by perpetual drunkard parents. At sixteen I, was drinking Chang'aa, the illicit brew that my mother was making and selling to the villagers. I was abusing drugs which I was introduced to by my friend Kim.

I started abusing drugs as fun, but later, I was hooked and addicted. In 1976, my parents relocated in Kiambogo settlement farm in Elementaita.Life in the up country was very different for me. I decided to try farming by enduring drought, crop failure and famine because of climate change. I hustled up for food, jobs and burnt charcoal to feed my siblings.

I was tired of living in such a miserable life. That's when my friend gave me a book by Billy Graham. The title was, World Aflame. When I was reading the book, Gods redeeming love arrested me, as the scriptures convicted my heart and spirit. I was unable to restrain tears from welling up in my eyes. I knelt down beside my bed in my small cube and asked Jesus Christ to save me from my sins. I was saved and transformed.

After salvation, I joined full Gospel Church in the village. The pastor was teaching from Acts 1.8...." But, you shall receive power, after that the Holy Spirit will come upon you, and you shall be my witnesses both in Jerusalem, and in all Judea, and in Samaria, and unto the uttermost part of the earth. "I believed the word of God and when I was praising God at the end of the service I felt power in my spirit.

Later I was filled in the Holy Spirit and I spoke in tongues. God became very real in my life. As I was growing up spiritually, I started experiencing the call of God in my life. In 1990, I was appointed a full time pastor and posted in Gilgil local church. I married Mary in the church and God blessed us with three children who are adults working in different parts in our country. In the year 2000, I registered Gospel Messengers Church. And in the year 2014, I was appointed as a Bishop of our ministry. Praise God. This book is about my story, how God transformed me from a hustler to a Bishop. God is using me in a wonderful way to reaching the unreached and in giving hope to the hopes in this hurting world.

I have a ministry of hope. Glory to God! This is a great challenge and a tower of strength to the hopeless. The ministry should be the place where troubled souls automatically find hope. It should be a place where they can turn for help, fellowship, wisdom, joy, and rest in their souls. One of the most substantial parts of my ministry is building happy and fulfilling Christian families.

Troubled people are looking for answers to their problems. Jesus is the answer to all of your problems. The ministry is like a hospital for all those who are sick physically, mentally, emotionally, and spiritually. The ministry is a father to those who are fatherless, a mother to those who have no mother, and a home to the homeless. Needy people appreciate those who can celebrate with them during their times of trials and needs.

God has called upon me to give hope to the hurting. Are you assaulted, abused, rejected, or abandoned? I am here to encourage you; there is hope for you in Jesus Christ.

I am praying God to raise many church leaders who will be messengers of hope together with me in this ministry to the needy. We need anointed Gospel messengers who will be willing to go out to where the sinners are. As messengers, we will be prepared to stand up and speak openly about the hurting issues in our society.

However, let us not despair, because the Bible warns that, "There will be terrible times in the last days" (2 Tim. 3:14). That's why our enemy —the devil—"is filled with fury because he knows that his time is short" (Rev. 12:10–12).

We have a Christian way of reaching out to the needy in love because we are members of Christ's body in Africa; we are Christ's hands, feet, and mouth. Jesus meets needy people through us. He saves, heals, and comforts the suffering through our mouths. He lovingly touches them using our hands. Although we cannot solve all the problems in this world, we are called to give ourselves to help the needy. Jesus wants us to show mercy to them. The word of God says — "For I desire mercy and not sacrifice" (Matt. 9:13).

I am called to minister to the whole man, spirit, body, and soul. We encourage Gospel Messengers Church, to be involved in community development in Africa. Some of the church leaders believe that physical development is unspiritual and worldly. Jesus is the light of the world in all things. We are called to care about the welfare of the needy in our society.

We are chosen by God to be channels of blessings to the needy. We are to allow God's love to flow into others by performing acts of mercy. God has promised abundant blessings to all those who minister to the needy. The mission field starts at your doorstep. True compassion is love in action. Let's just do it! God's love is not given through our emotions, but rather our action; it would be doing something. Caring for the needy does not mean preaching to them anointed sermons; it means helping them in love. The Bible says, "Owe no man anything but love" (Rom. 13:8).

While ministering to the needy, we have seen God changing their lives. Change in behavior begins with a change in their hearts. We preach the gospel to the needy, and we pray with those who have a variety of problems. Wherever we go to minister to the needy we see the evidence of the Word changing people as they become good Christians. Needy people come to our office for prayer. After receiving the answer to their prayers, they invite us into their homes to share the word of God with their families, friends, and neighbors. I minister comfort as we minister to needy people with great crises and problems in their lives.

We are soon starting a project to help those with disabilities by enhancing their quality of life. If such people can be supported, they can become successful citizens. We are thanking God for the many families who are being reunited. Sick bodies have been healed, and relationships restored. We are making a difference in this evil society. I have compassion and a consuming desire to minister to the poor, the needy, widows, HIV/AIDS victims, orphans, and street children. It is time for us to stop floundering around being preoccupied with our agendas and problems. There is a fire that cannot be quenched that is burning in my heart to minister to the needy.

The ministry is willing to take immediate action to alleviate poverty and improve the living conditions of the destitute in the slums and in the ghettos. We are eager to provide the basic necessities of survival for the impoverished.

Let me ask you a question—have you ever seen a slum or a ghetto in your life? If you have never visited a slum, let me briefly explain to you what a slum is. A slum is an area where thousands of poverty-stricken people live together in a crowded village in deplorable conditions. These destitute people live in the unhealthiest and uncomfortable conditions.

Many of these slum dwellers are jobless, and so they struggle to provide for their families. Some of their women survive by making and selling the illicit brew known as "Kumi Kumi." Many of the slum dwellers like to escape their problems in the drink. However, they would wake up the next morning with the same issues; if not more.

Slum houses are made of polythene walls, which have changed their color because of accumulated dirt on the walls and roof. At night you can see the light flickering from kerosene lamps or candles in the homes.

In various corners of the village, you could meet with some of the many idle, pale-faced, ill-nourished, and stunted slum dwellers. Many of these people go to sleep with empty stomachs. Most nights are dreary experiences for many of them.

It is dangerous to walk alone in the slums if you are a stranger. Gangs of drug-addicted criminals could easily attack you. Many jobless young men roam in these areas doing criminal and demonic activities. These armed gangs of young men create danger in every corner of the slums. Rates of drug abuse, alcoholism, prostitution, and crime are very high in these areas. These evil ways of life affect the minds of the victims, causing them to become involved in stealing, raping, fighting, and doing any kind of evil thing they can imagine.

Because of increased crime, people live there in fear. Everybody living there indeed has a terrible story to tell. Many slum dwellers are destitute and many sleep on the floor with cheap mattresses and some tattered beddings, which are packed together in a corner after use. Another terrible thing is that human waste can be seen openly in every empty space in the slums. During the day, the smell becomes strong, and during the rainy season, it is a dangerous health hazard, as rainwater carries it to all parts of the slum.

In this area, society's real problem is the problem of the heart. Although we are living in the most sophisticated world of information and high technology, our national reputation is marred by these increasing problems of racial prejudice, divorce, drug addiction, sexual immorality, prostitution, alcoholism, crime, and violence. These problems are all experienced in the slums. They are caused by poverty that has been passed from generation to generation. Many of our problems come from within the heart. The Bible says, "For out of the heart proceed evil thoughts, thefts, false witnesses, blasphemies... These are the things that defile a man" (Matt. 15:19–20).

The gospel is needed in these areas because there is the problem of unwanted children. This is a severe problem. Parents get distraught upon witnessing a young girl giving birth outside of marriage. They consider the birth of such a child as another burden on the family. In slums, many children are born outside of marriage and are treated as unwanted. They are rejected, and they end up in the streets where they would become dangerous street kids.

Other families have many children without planning. The children often become a burden to the family. Why should we not consider every child who is born in every family as a blessing? It is because many don't want to plan in order to have the number of children they would be able to handle. People need to have control of the number of children they want to have in their family to avoid the possibility of the children running away from home.

We have the problem of abortion because people consider abortion a form of birth control. Abortion is the act of destroying the fetus in the womb before it is born. Birth control is planning to have only the number of children you can feed, clothe, and take to school.

I have realized that in our ministry to the needy, the first thing to do is to alleviate poverty in the lives of the slum dwellers. This can alleviate some pressures and allow them to be sensitive to the gospel of Jesus Christ, who died for their sins. We are prepared to live out of our comfort zones to meet the needs of the needy who are suffering in the slums and ghettos.

I know the little we can give is very important in the hands of the needy. The Bible says, "I was a father to the poor" (Job 29:16). Remember how Mary anointed Jesus with her costly oil? It was considered by Jesus to be very significant and expensive. So, give to the needy at least some of life's necessities that you have. God is our provider, so don't be afraid to share with others in need. The Bible says, "Have you seen anyone perish for the need of clothing or any poor without covering?" (Job 31:9). God is willing to use you for His divine purposes if you are willing to share with others whatever little He has given you. Be a good steward of whatever God has given you. Just begin to give sacrificial gifts. We are messengers of hope in this hurting world.

I know that the short-term relief we give the needy or the poor is not enough. We must provide them with the gospel because it has the power to change them from within. The gospel is like a sweet-smelling fragrance in the noses of the sinners in the slums. We are living letters that speak well of our Lord Jesus Christ in this hurting world.

A good deed is like medicine to the needy, so let's perform acts of mercy to them. Actions speak more eloquently than empty words. We are called to bring the hopeless into the presence of God, where they can find new hope, new life, joy, and peace in their lives. In Jesus Christ, there is satisfaction, and you can never thirst or hunger anymore. Let's be faithful in helping others because God will pay us back richly for every penny we have used for His divine purpose. The Bible says, "Therefore, as we were opportunity, let us do good to all, especially to those who are of the household of Faith" (Gal. 5:10).

You can now visualize the actual picture of the destitute slum dwellers. Join us in making a difference in their hurting lives. Your prayers and finances will help us to build a relief project in the slums. Join us in forming a robust, crusading army of compassion that will be marching towards the slums to help the needy. These impoverished people need caring people who will help them fight the evil forces of sins, diseases, and poverty in their troubled lives. This is a wonderful story with a strong appeal. Just try to listen to the cry of the poor in the slums, "Africa belongs to Jesus." Let this be your cry, too.

I have discovered that when you minister to the basic needs of the hungry or the poor, the gospel is easily accepted in the community. We have a life-changing project that is trying to address the famine crisis in our country. The weather patterns have changed, causing crop failures, which result in many people starving to death. We are trying to reach out in love, despite our limited economic conditions in this ministry.

Remember that a few years ago, we had been looking at very frightening pictures of people starving to death in countries like Ethiopia, Sudan, Somalia, and other parts of Africa. But now, we have experienced famine in some areas of Kenya. Our ministry is trying to do what it can to save the famine victims in the Rift Valley, Eastern, Northeast, and Coast Province in Kenya.

We must do something to save lives. We have created a channel for sharing information and resources in our office in Nairobi. We are planning to start feeding programs and healthcare services in the famine-hit areas and in the slums.

I was born in a poverty-stricken ghetto, and so I know what it means to be hungry and malnourished. For this reason, the famine victims are in my heart, and their needs stay in my mind. I do consider every human being as God's perfect creation, with equal rights to life's abundant provisions, irrespective of race, color, or geographic location.

We are helping the desperate farmers start their farming business again for their survival. It is time to think, as a Christian organization, about how we can make an impact on this hurting society. We are very willing to use locally available resources in our lives. We are trying to promote the farmers by giving them some farm implements, seeds, and fertilizers.

Many people are suffering without much food as a result of famine and floods. Millions of innocent people who have been working in their farms find themselves starving as they flee elsewhere to find food and other necessities of survival. That is why our humanitarian projects are creating developing plans aimed at transforming many lives. We are trying to use efficient and effective ways to reach out in love. We are responsible for helping the hungry people with food because the specter of famine that leads to death is worrisome to me. We are not going to spare our resources to achieve our goals for the common good.

We have reports filtering in from our Christian workers who tell us how people are starving due to crop failure. People find themselves in precarious situations. Food shortages have caused many deaths and much misery in Kenya. That is why we are appealing to the generous people around the world to help us with food donations.

Remember that drought comes unexpectedly and so often. The tragedy is that we are unable to take measures to stop it because of a lack of material resources or finances. We are living in a world of uncertainty because seasons have changed, situations have changed, and conditions have changed. However, we have hope in the truth that "Jesus is the same yesterday, today, and forever" (Heb. 13:8).

Our ministry is revisiting the whole question of famine and has developed precise strategies to help avoid scarcity in the future. The weather patterns have changed beyond our control, but we are expecting God to help the farmers plant when the weather is favorable. We appeal to our brothers and sisters in other parts of the world to help in this famine crisis. It is good to help starving people with food and then educate them on how to overcome such situations in the future.

We are concerned with the plight of the starving people. Our evangelism must address all aspects of a human being. The Bible tells us to share our daily bread with the needy and cover the naked. We believe in God to assist us in helping the hungry because God promises special blessings to the ones who care.

Remember. Africa does not need more religions when millions of people are suffering without something to eat. We don't need more mega-church buildings while our religious leaders are ignoring the people's basic needs. We need to help the needy and portray Jesus Christ in their lives by loving them through our actions, just like the disciples. The disciples preached with the anointing and cared for the needy and the widows.

The apostle, Paul, had a ministry to the poor. When the disciples cared for the needy and the poor, the gospel was accepted, and the church increased in number. The Word of God says, "If you draw out your soul to the hungry and satisfy the afflicted soul, then your light will rise in drought and make fat your bones. You shall be like a watered garden and like a spring of water, whose waters fail not" (Isa. 58:10–11). We are willing to help the starving in whatever capacity we might be able to, be it through prayer or the sharing of our resources.

Jesus is the answer. He is ready to save your life from sins and the present inner pain in your hurting soul. Maybe you are desperate and feel unable to cope with a situation, and you could be thinking that nobody is caring for you. Call Jesus, because He died for your sins, and He is your best friend.

I am a messenger of hope and caring for your life. I have a word of encouragement, a smile, and a caring heart. I have prayed for sinners and hopeless people. I have seen troubled lives move on with peace in their hearts after receiving Jesus Christ in their souls. I have seen troubled and sick people receiving their healing after praying for them by faith in Jesus's name. I have seen troubled families restored after prayer in Jesus's name. No one whose hope is in Jesus Christ is hopeless!

Question: Do you have any problems in your life now? Do you have in your life any hurting wound in your heart that is bleeding and very painful? Do you have any spiritual or physical problems? Do you have a grief that you don't know how to resolve? Do you have an ache in your soul? Come now to Jesus Christ with all of your sins, diseases, pains, aches, sufferings, grief's, troubles, problems, and burdens. The Bible says, "Come to me, all who are weary and burdened, and I will give you rest" (Matt.11:28).

Jesus Christ was crucified on the cross for you and me. The Bible says that when He was on the cross, "Surely He has borne our griefs, and carried our sorrows, yet we esteemed him stricken, smitten by God, and afflicted, but He was wounded for our transgressions, He was bruised for our iniquities, and upon Him the chastisement that made us whole, and with His stripes we are healed" (Isa.53:4–5).

Rejoice that we have a caring father like Jesus in our lives today. He is the king of peace in our souls. He is ready and willing to provide for our needs. We are part of His divine flock, and we can say, "The Lord is our shepherd." Jesus is ready to pour healing oil of the Holy Spirit in every deep hurt in our lives. The Bible says, "For I will restore health unto thee and I will heal thee of thy wounds, Saith the Lord" (Jer. 30:17).

Jesus is willing to save you, heal you, and deliver you from your present problems now. Do you want to be saved, healed, or delivered? I am praying and pleading on your account in the throne of grace in heaven. Let this be a word in time to receive Jesus Christ now as your personal savior. Then promise to join a good Bible-believing church in your area and start serving your God there with other believers.

You have a clear picture of what salvation, healing, and deliverance is all about. Hell is a place of everlasting torment with unquenchable fire. Hell is not made for you. A clear picture of hell can make you decide to receive Jesus Christ as your personal savior. Jesus is coming soon! The hour of His coming is at hand. Surely this is your time to seek salvation—after this—?

"When they shall be saying peace and safety suddenly destruction cometh" (1 Thess. 5:3). Fear not; only believe! Remember that medical science has failed to provide treatment for some diseases like HIV/AIDS, but Jesus heals every disease. Why don't you call upon Him and see? Jesus is the answer!

The moment you receive Jesus Christ in your heart, all the promised blessings in God's word begin to flow into your life. The secret to overcoming the world is believing in Jesus Christ. He is coming to take us home to Heaven, where the Bible says that "They shall neither hunger any more nor thirst anymore; the sun shall not strike them, nor any heat; for the Lord who is in the midst of the throne will shepherd them and lead them in living fountains of waters, And God will wipe away every tear from their eyes" (Rev. 7:16–17).

Jesus is our savior and our great physician. Nothing is impossible with Him. The main objective of this ministry to the needy is to take people to a new level of victory over sin and disease. To make them whole in the body, soul, and spirit.

Ever since the Lord called me into the ministry, I have been leading thousands of hopeless people to Jesus Christ. I build their hope in the anchor and in the strong foundation in Christ. I tell the hopeless to build on this unshakable foundation that never moves. I tell the needy to put their trust on the Rock of all ages, Jesus Christ. In Him, you can keep on living in this troubled world, even when the storms persist. When life in this troubled world seems harsh, in Jesus we find refuge.

We are living in evil times of war and uncertainty, but Jesus is giving us peace during these storms of life. I preach hope to all those who are living in desperation, for we are living in an era of trouble. I am standing up to tell all people in this troubled world to amend their ways and repent their sins; and to receive Jesus Christ in their hearts. Jesus is the Prince of Peace, and He is able to end all wars and conflicts in the world.

I'm a messenger of hope who is preaching God's unfailing love, grace, mercy, and forgiveness. Amid affliction, I speak hope. Let me encourage you. You could be nearly at the end, or perhaps you are just about to hit the bottom, but I can assure you that no matter what, there is hope for you. Don't look at the failures. You are going to let Jesus Christ save you now.

Just invite Jesus into your heart now, and you will get all you need. You can receive what you are longing for in your heart. Jesus is the answer! I invite you to come to our church, and you will get a message of hope from the Messenger of Hope. In this book you read my true story of how God transformed me from a hustler to a Bishop.

Chapter 5

A DREAM OF HOPE

Many nations, especially the third-world countries, are experiencing economic pressures caused by political corruption and greed. We have many floods, earthquakes, and famines, which are caused by what they are calling "global warming." Millions of people today are being affected by what has been happening in Africa.

As a messenger of God, I am deeply affected by these harsh conditions in this hurting world. I know what the Bible says: "Nation will rise against nation...there will be famines, and earthquakes in various places — many will turn away from the faith, and many false prophets will appear and deceive many people, and because of the increase of wickedness, the love of most people will grow cold" (Matt. 24:7–12).

God's word has much to say about the last days. My focus, however, was very much upon the evil things that were taking place in our country concerning election violence and tribal clashes. Kenya experienced turmoil a few years ago when many people slashed their neighbors with pangas, spears, and arrows, just like goats. People were suffering and perishing with nowhere to turn for help.

An epidemic of violence plagues our villages, towns, and cities with armed gangs of attackers who are killing people, looting, raping, and destroying property. Women and young girls are raped and molested openly, while others are killed. Families are perishing.

As a messenger of hope, I have encouraged the victims of violence and rape. I read to them the Word, that says, "I will not die but live and declare the works of the Lord" (Ps. 118:17). I called their attention to what the scriptures teach in this regard. I have encouraged them to hope and trust in God. Jesus said, "Because I live, you shall also live" (John 14:19).

In Jesus Christ, we have hope for survival. My vision is to give hope for survival to the hopeless. My ministry is for encouraging and strengthening the victims who had been displaced or disowned.

While some people in this world are philosophically discussing where we are in the end-time events, others are suffering and perishing without hope for survival. These are the last days. Let us wake up and help the needy and the hopeless before it is too late.

Let us repent of our sins and gently accept Jesus Christ as our personal Savior. Let us preach the gospel as never before and warn the world about the coming destruction.

Let us tell all people that Jesus is coming soon, and only those of righteousness will be saved. My vision is to give hope to the hopeless. Let me tell you-with Jesus Christ, survival is possible.

The nations of the world are busy trying to find natural solutions to the dangers that are all around them. But it is only Jesus, and Him alone, who can give answers to all the problems of this hurting world.

Jesus knows of all the problems that we are experiencing because He experienced the same problems when He was here in this world. In the Bible, we read that problems started immediately for Jesus because Herod, the king at that time, wanted to kill Jesus. The living God appeared to Joseph, the father of Jesus, in a dream and urged the holy family to flee immediately to Egypt (Africa). Joseph obeyed the voice of God and left for Egypt.

The Lord appeared to Joseph in a dream and said, "Rise and take the child and his mother, and flee to Egypt and remain their till I tell you; for Herod is about to search for the child to destroy him" (Matt. 2:13–14). So, Joseph rose and took the child and mother that night and departed to Egypt.

Herod killed all young children in Israel, for he was searching through them all to find and kill Jesus. The Bible says, "A voice was heard in Raman, wailing and loud lamentation — Rachel weeping for her children; she refused to be consoled because they were no more" (Matt. 2:18).

The holy family was saved in Egypt, Africa. That's why I believe what Dr. Morris Cerullo says: "Africa belongs to Jesus." God loves Africa, and He has a good plan for Africa. Joseph saved his family by obeying the voice of God in his dream. This was a dream of hope.

I will always remember the day the Lord appeared to me in a soul-thrilling dream. Many years ago, I was preaching the gospel as a full-time pastor in the Kiambogo village in Elementaita. Every day I was busy winning souls for Christ in the village. I was always feeding myself spiritually from the word of God and always praying for the needy and the hopeless. I prayed continually, and therefore I lived a life free of care while doing what I loved most: preaching the gospel in the village.

I loved serving the Lord in the ministry, even though we had no church building. We held our Sunday service meetings under a big tree every Sunday. The church members walked every Sunday morning across about ten to seven kilometers to attend the services. The members were mainly farmers, and for some years they had experienced drought. They had no food to give to their families, let alone giving their offerings to God. As their pastor, I was struggling to survive in the ministry.

I was influential in the ministry, despite experiencing a lot of difficulties with my family in the village church. I used to call Jesus in prayer to heal my situation and that of the ministry at large. Are you experiencing problems in your life? Could you be suffering hurt or an injury in your heart or spirit? The Bible has an answer for your case: "Your wound is incurable, your injury beyond healing. There is no remedy for your sore; no healing for you" (Jer. 30:12–13).

My situation looked hopeless. I cried to God day and night to heal and restore me. I had hope, however, even though I was wounded in my heart. I was desperate and kept on calling Jesus to help me.

The Word of God encouraged me, "Out of the depths I cry to you, o lord, o lord, hear my voice. Let your ears be attentive to my cry for mercy. If you, o lord, kept the cord of sins, o Lord, who could stand? But with you there is forgiveness. Therefore, you are feared. I wait for the Lord; my soul waits, and in His word I put my hope. My soul waits for the Lord more than watchmen waiting for the morning. O Israel, put your hope in the Lord, for within the Lord is unfailing love and with Him is full redemption" (Ps. 130:1–7).

I was a full-time pastor, but downcast in my soul. I was disturbed within myself. I was asking myself, "How long, Lord?" I was desperate, like the prophet, Elijah. When he sat down under a tree, he prayed that he might die (1 Kings 19:4–5).

I believed God was able to heal and restore my wounded heart. The word of God encouraged my heart. Put your hope in God, for

I will praise Him, my Savior, and my God (Psalms 42:5). I decided to seek the Lord in prayer through fasting for five days. "My tears have been my food day and night while they continually say to me, 'Where [is] your God?'" (Ps. 42:3).

God reminded me of a soul-thrilling dream I experienced many years ago. In the dream, I saw the Lord Almighty in His great throne. To me, this was a direct revelation of El Shaddai, the Great I Am. He was splendid, majestic, and so magnificent. As I looked, I was awestruck by His presence and glory. I wanted to stay in His presence, for I was encountering His wonderful radiance of power and glory.

Before me, there was a picture of a map of Africa shaped like a question mark. In it, I saw millions of sinners; the needy and hopeless faces of black people from all nations of Africa. They looked very frustrated, for they were suffering from all kinds of calamities, famines, diseases, tragedies, civil wars, conflicts, tribal clashes, and financial crises.

As I looked, I heard a voice that said, "God, reach these hurting souls." I then suddenly woke up with a burning memory of this awesome dream in my mind. The dream to me was two-fold. Firstly, I was to reach the unreached. Secondly, preach hope to the hopeless. Since then, Africa has been in my heart, and the world in my mind.

"The Lord put out His hand and touched my mouth, and the Lord said unto me, 'Behold. I have this day sent you over the nations and over kingdoms to root out and pull down, to build and plant'" (Jer. 1:9–10).

My soul was healed, and the promise in the word of God was real in my heart: "I will restore health to you, and I will heal your wounds" (Jer. 30:17).

The Lord had shown me a dream of hope for the hopeless in Africa. I felt love and compassion for the poor, the needy, the sinners, and the suffering in this hurting world.

The Lord sent me out to reach the unreached and to preach hope to the hopeless. I was made a messenger of hope in Africa. I ministered hope to the members of my church in the village. I preached powerful messages of hope and encouragement. The members rejoiced, and they sang songs of praise to our God. The church was revived, and it increased in number daily.

I preached with new hope for survival. I overcame all trials and temptations. My family and my ministry were never the same again. I was completely changed. I was doing God's will in my life through the leading of the Holy Spirit. The Sunday services and the midweek fellowships were not the same anymore, either. The church increased with new faces of men, women, and youth. Even the backsliders returned to God.

I had no savings, and I survived on a hand-to-mouth basis. My family started to experience a breakthrough in our finances. The Lord became omnipotent in our lives, and He was providing for our needs. That's why I said, "I will always hope in Him." I will hope in Him even when all things seem impossible, because in Him, all things are possible.

God intervened in my life and in the ministry. He blessed me and the ministry both. The ministry was growing. Job's life served as a great encouragement to me. God created a great future out of my miserable situation. My circumstances were terrible, but God restored me.

Job said of His life, "My spirit is broken, my days are cut short, the grave awaits me—my eyes have drowned him with grief; my eyes have grown dim with grief; my whole frame is but a shadow—my days have passed; my plans shattered and so are the desires of my heart—where then is hope: who can see any hope for me? Will it go down the gates of death? Will we descend together into dust?" (Job 17:1–16).

I have said, like Job, that I will not lose hope, but rather I will trust in the Lord of my salvation. Job said, "Though he slays me yet will I hope in Him" (Job 13:15). Because Job trusted the Lord completely without wavering, he was rewarded. "The Lord made him prosperous again and gave him twice as much as he had before" (Job 42:10). "The Lord blessed the latter part of Job's life more than the first" (Job 42:12).

The word of God encouraged me, "For I know the plans I have for you, plans to give you hope and a future. Then you will call upon me and come and pray to me, and I will listen to you. You will seek me and find me when you seek me with all your heart" (Jeremiah 29:10–13).

My struggles and my problems were meant to tear me down, but God restored me. Since the day the Lord appeared unto me in a dream, hope for that picture of people suffering has been deeply etched in my heart.

I tell all people with problems there is hope through acceptance in Christ. I ask them to put their trust in God. It's only God who has the power to make you live or die. He can save, heal, deliver, restore, renew, forgive, guide, comfort, encourage, strengthen, provide, and open doors for you. He is our God who says, "Behold. I am the Lord, the God of all flesh. Is there anything too hard for me?" (Jer. 32:27).

I encourage the needy to trust in God, and they will find joy for their salvation. The Bible says, "May the God of Hope fill you with all joy and peace as you trust in Him, so that you may overflow with hope by the power of the Holy Spirit" (Rom. 15:13).

What a blessed privilege it is to share with you my divine dream. I believe God has beautiful plans for those who are suffering from diseases, tribal clashes, and famines in Africa. I'm not making this statement based on who you are, but rather on what the Lord has said to us in the Bible. No matter how terrible your situation could be, God cares for your needs, and He has good plans for your life.

God created you, and He loves you. He wants you to have the best. He wants your life to be filled with joy, peace, and purpose. Expect great things to happen in your life as you look to God. "And God [is] able to make all grace abound toward you, that you, always having all sufficiency in all [things], may have an abundance for every good work" (2 Cor. 9:8).

God is able to do all great things in your life that you can ask or imagine, according to His power that is at work within us (Eph 3:20). God gave Pharaoh a dream of hope, and Joseph interpreted the dream (Genesis 41:25). Egypt was saved from famine.

We have every reason to look forward to spiritual blessings because God has given us all grace. God saves, redeems, protects, and restores. Why not call upon Him now? That's why we are living a life worthy of the Lord. We want to please Him in every way and bear fruit in every good work. Let us maintain endurance and patience as we trust in Him.

God is working in Africa as never before. He is working in our lives. The life of Job is a good illustration of how the Lord works, even though he had experienced great adversity in his life. God blessed the latter part of Job's life more than the first (Job 42:12).

No matter what the condition of your present situation may be, the Lord has good plans for your life. Never lose hope. Trust in God and put your confidence in Him.

Our ministry is counting on years of His faithfulness, and the impact is only going to increase in the days ahead. We are rejoicing to be able to reach the unreached and give hope to the hopeless in this hurting world.

We are thanking all those who have been willing to give this ministry their kind support and help us in making a difference in this hurting world. Your support will help us in making this dream of hope a reality.

Through Jesus Christ, I have hope for survival, for He said, "Because I live you will live also" (John 14:19). I have a dream of hope for Africa. I believe what Dr. Morris Cerullo says: "Africa belongs to Christ."

I am declaring — Africa, awake! Arise! And shine! With Jesus Christ, survival is possible!

Chapter 6

AFRICA IN MY HEART

I became a Christian in Kiambogo Village, Gilgil District, Nakuru County, in 1978. After my salvation, I started writing Gospel articles and gave them to my friends, relatives, and neighbors. After they read the gospel messages, some asked to be saved and joined my church.

Kiambogo Village is about forty-five kilometers from Nakuru Town and almost thirty-five kilometers from Gilgil Town. It is surrounded by Eburu Forest on the East, and Mau Forest on the West. Eburu Forest is famous for being the home of bongo, buffalo, and many other wild animals, including many species of birds. In the village at night, you could often hear herds of buffalo from the forest invading our crops. That is why our village was named after the word, "Kiambogo," meaning "a village of many buffalos."

During the dry seasons, there is an acute shortage of water. Dams and rivers are often dry due to prolonged drought. Women and children suffer because they are forced to wake up very early and walk long distances in search of water.

In 1985, the Lord visited me in a vision. I saw the Almighty Lord on the great throne in Heaven. Before me, there was a picture of a map of Africa, which was shaped like a question mark. I described the picture of the people on the map previously. Many of the people looked very disappointed, frustrated, hungry, hopeless, and hurting; some of them were weeping helplessly.

As I looked, transfixed, I was awestruck by God's presence and glory. I saw the hand of God moving as never before saving, healing, and changing the whole continent of Africa. *Africa belongs to God*, I thought. A voice spoke, "Go! Reach the unreached with the gospel of faith, love, and hope." I then suddenly woke up with a vivid memory of that awesome vision from heaven. That's when I said, like Paul, "...I was not disobedient to the heavenly vision" (Acts 26:19).

God had appeared to me in a vision and confirmed to me that my vision and ministry is to reach the unreached in Africa. I started open-air meetings and crusades in different parts of our country. Today the ministry has spread even to the neighboring countries.

Since that wonderful day of my visitation, Africa has been in my heart and the Word in my mind. I have agreed to obey my vision to the end and to go everywhere to preach the gospel as the Lord leads. I have taken my vision and the task that was designated to me by God very seriously. I promised God that I would carry my vision forward without reservations.

Before my inner eyes were opened by God, I was about to drown in fear, anxiety, and uncertainty about my life and ministry. Suddenly, when I was praying one night, God visited me in my vision. Today I am busy preaching the gospel in East and Central Africa. I am helping to build the body of Christ in Africa with other ministers of the Gospel. I am teaching ministers how to focus on their visions and ministries.

Please read my book, *Obeying My Vision*. You will be built up and strengthened to focus on your vision and ministry. God assured me that my testing and provision are both part of my vision. I have declared, like the apostle, Paul, that, "I was not disobedient to the heavenly vision" (Acts 26:19*)*. I will obey my vision.

Write your vision

THE BIBLE TELLS US to write our vision very clearly and make it very plain. "Write the vision and make it plain on tables, that he may run who read it" (Hab. 2:2). Joseph is an excellent example of a vision bearer who wrote his vision clearly. He wrote how God visited him in two different dreams. However, the time came when he started struggling and suffering for his dream or vision. It took years before his vision was fulfilled, and it required him to become a slave and later to spend many years in jail to prepare him for what God was going to do in his life. That is to say; there is no vision without pain. Read Genesis chapter 37, 39–41.

That's why I'm focusing on my vision in preaching the gospel, as well as making myself available so that God can use me in meeting hurting people's needs. I am willing to seek God's will in my life and ministry. That's why I am reading God's word and praying every day. I'm willing to go out and help the hopeless, despite knowing that they have nothing with which to repay me.

Chapter 7

GIVING HOPE TO THE HOPELESS

The Bible is the ultimate book of hope, in that with God, everything is possible. With Him, every weed can be made a potential rose. It is the Bible that tells us that Jonah, the prophet, got a second chance to go back to Nineveh, and the whole city turned to God (Jonah 3:1–10). The Bible also tells us of the prodigal son who came from a wasted life and was restored to his family (Luke 15:11–24).

What about the story of Peter, the disciple who denied Christ but later became the greatest leader in the New Testament church and died as a martyr for the cause of Christ? If you want to become great in God's Kingdom, just be an encouragement, nurturer, and restorer of the hurting and the hopeless. God will reward you in Heaven.

The Bible says that "pleasant words are healing..." (Prov. 16–24). Do you build others up with your words, encouraging and restoring them, or do you tear them down? How do people feel when they are around you? Do they feel inferior or insignificant, or do they feel great and important?

God called us to encourage the hurting and the hopeless in this troubled world.

Be an encourager. Have the heart to give hope through encouraging others by telling them to keep on trying until they make it. God is looking for encouragers and restorers in His kingdom.

Most of us have no idea that what we say builds others up emotionally and spiritually.

The opposite of encouraging is spreading discouragement. Do not let any kind of discouragement come out from your mouth. Speak faith, love, and hope to all the hurting and the hopeless in your life. Build others and let them benefit from your words of encouragement and restoration.

Words of discouragement can leave scars for a lifetime. People will never forget something you have said to them, and that includes criticism and rebuke. So, make the best possible use of words so that they can bless others. Ask God to make you an encourager, and you will be a blessing to others.

As a pastor, I like to choose a message to encourage the members of my church. As a dad to my three children, I love to encourage and appreciate them. I teach them how to maintain a close relationship with our heavenly father. At home, I make sure that they feel loved. God's love will always outgrow. More than anything else, I have discovered that my children want to be loved. There is no difference between the sexes; both want to feel loved.

God has given me a ministry of loving and encouraging orphans and vulnerable children. I want to be their dad, their role model, and their pastor. I am delighted to encourage them as I share my life with them. I share my values, my priorities, and what I stand for in my life. They need to know God's plans for their lives. I teach them that Christianity is something to be enjoyed and not to be endured.

Look at the problems of child abuse, which has caused millions of children to flee from their homes and families and end up living on the streets in towns and cities all over the world. Some parents mistreat their children. Others reject them. Either way, the kids end up on the streets. And as they grow up on the streets, many become very dangerous criminals in order to survive.

Some of these children rejected by their parents become criminals in schools and colleges. They cause chaos, strikes, and disruptions, and they damage school resources. Many people in towns or cities are crying foul because of the mess that is created by these disowned kids in the streets.

Our young daughters today are getting pregnant at an early age, and that is why we have a lot of these street children in community. That's why many people in the nations are asking, "What's the most effective way of helping our young girls from becoming pregnant, and the most effective way of helping the millions of these babies they are having?" To some of these girls, the answer seems fairly obvious. They will tell you, "We need help, or else we are going to have an abortion."

In some parts of the world, because of hard times and economics, we are hearing stories of an increase of millions of disowned children in the streets. That's why we are hearing of an increase in murder, rape, defilement, theft, burglary, pick-pocketing, and criminal gangs in the streets at night.

As a minister of the gospel working together with other stakeholders, we are finding the most effective way to address these increasing problems. We have all of what it takes to treasure and care for every disowned kid in this world. We can do forums locally or internationally and find ways to address the emerging problem of disowned kids.

I focus on every disowned child positively. I love children, and that's why I'm very concerned with these disowned kids. I'm working hard to find ways of connecting with the right people who have a burden to help these helpless kids in society. Could you please join hands with us and consider that every child is precious before God?

The ministry to support these disowned kids is very hard and costly. It takes a lot of my time, resources, and emotions to care for each child. I tell families to value these kids and not to disown them. Every child is a gift from God. Read Psalms 139:13–14: "You knit me together in my mother's womb. I praise you because I am fearfully and wonderfully made."

Many nations and families in the world are dealing with population-related issues. A country like China handles children with great care and great efficiency. Under the Chinese government, there is the "one-child-per-family" policy. Only the first child is considered legal by the government.

Other nations have formed laws restricting the number of children who can be born in a family. Under the law, any couple expecting an extra child is forced to abort them. Because of increased financial problems in our homes, families are admiring these laws that control childbirth in the nations.

Would you like your local leaders to pass these laws of birth control? Would you want a law to be passed allowing abortion on demand? As for me, as a minister of the gospel, I will never support any type of abortion unless the life of the mother is in danger.

I know some families are doing abortions by choice because they believe that an unplanned child is a burden. Others think they can get rid of a girl child because she would just be a burden, whereas boys would be more valuable. There are those families who genuinely believe this. As a servant of God, I am teaching families the value of every child. There are right ways of bringing up every child with God's help.

The Bible encourages us that we are fearfully and wonderfully made. When I look at a street kid, I see a moving miracle in the street. I see a fearfully and wonderfully made child by God. I see God's own handwork. God is the reason for every birth, including yours.

While some nations are enjoying the fruits of modern technology, their birth control policies have caused them to have a very small number of children or teenagers.

Let's look at these birth control policies with a new focus because we can cause trouble for ourselves. No new technologies can match the miracle of a child. Let's not take the birth of any child for granted. What I can say is that it's not wrong to have children but don't have too many. God has given you the capacity to plan.

I don't support killing some so that others can enjoy life. I will never ignore any child or person in the world. It's utterly immoral to think evil of any human being. We are all created in God's image. Let's therefore survive by helping others to survive.

The problem of short reasoning is leading people and nations into a disaster. Every day in the media, we are hearing of family crises. It's my prayer that God will help everyone who is born into this world to survive. Instead of seeing the increased population of the world as a problem, let's help meet the needs of the helpless and the hopeless in life.

Plan how you will keep your family. Living in this world without planning for your family could be devastating. Stop seeing street kids as a problem. Instead, find ways to end their problems. Let's look at ways that these helpless and hopeless kids can enrich society. Let's plan for them and use them as a blessing and not as a burden. Let us use love, faith, and wisdom to do something good to these kids. If we don't plan for them, they may plan evil on us so that they may survive.

You should know that there is a great difference between planning birth control and abortion. Birth control is deciding how to bring a new life into being, while abortion is choosing to destroy a life that already exists in the womb before birth.

God has given us brains to think and plan. When I married my wife, we planned to have three children. My firstborn is a daughter, the second-born is a daughter, and the third one is a son. We planned to have only three kids within at an interval of four years. National leaders should plan for the population of their country, while families should plan on how many children they should have. Every government should protect its citizens. Every father should protect his family. That's God's plan for our lives.

Let me admit that it's not easy to minister to the disowned children or street kids. But within all these challenges, God cares for us all. Therefore, we should care for others. We are giving answers to the cries of these hopeless children. With God, everything is possible, so let us depend on God to reach the disowned children through us.

Some NGOs are distributing condoms to our teenagers in the streets, in schools, and in colleges, but the more they provide teenagers with condoms, the more pregnancies and abortions they have.

Let us teach the dangers of premarital sex. Sex outside marriage is wrong. We should lead young children to Jesus Christ because He can save and set them free from all sorts of sins, bondage, and addiction.

The world is becoming like Rama. "In Rama was there a voice heard, lamentation, and weeping, and great mourning, Rachel weeping [for] her children, and would not be comforted, because they are not" (Matt. 2:18 KJV).

"Then Herod, when he saw that he was mocked of the wise men, was exceeding wroth, and sent forth and slew all the children who were in Bethlehem, and in all the coasts thereof, from two years old and under, according to the time which he had diligently enquired of the wise men" (Matt. 2:16 KJV).

It's only God who can save the world from the hands of the devil, who is killing lives every day. Children should be a blessing to be celebrated and not be considered burden. Instead of complaining because of the mess these disowned children are doing to us, let's help them survive in a good way.

People in towns and cities have cried because of these kids for too long. The morning has dawned in the lives of these kids. "Weeping may endure for a night, but joy comes in the morning" (Ps. 30:5).

As believers, we should be leading these kids towards heaven, where they can be helped forever, instead of letting them suffer in this hurting world. With God through Jesus Christ, they can live triumphantly.

I was once a hopeless drug addict, but when I turned my life to Jesus Christ, I was saved and transformed. My neighbors were astounded by my testimony because of the mess I was involved in. That's why today, I'm ready to help others to get to know Jesus Christ personally. I have given up my fears and went out to reach the unreached in the streets, highways, towns, and cities. I believe that with God, all these problems that are disturbing young kids will disappear in Jesus's name.

"The mountains shall depart and the hill be removed, but my kindness shall not depart from you nor shall my covenant of peace be removed, says the Lord, who has mercy on you" (Isa. 54:10).

Through God's grace, I will work to support these disowned children, believing that all mountains will be removed before me and that the results of my ministry will stand forever. I will minister love and hope to broken hearts. I believe every situation will change, but God will never change. I will therefore speak openly and without fear of contradiction. I will support the disowned children.

Are you crying tears of sorrow and pain because you have been disowned or rejected by your family? Relax and trust in God. Jesus is ready to save you, and He will wipe away your tears. Just believe and trust in Him.

I'm called to give hopeless kids a hug and a special touch of love. Real love can be demonstrated through helping the needy. In our outreach ministry to these disowned children, we are giving them life-changing messages from the Bible, and we help them to receive Jesus Christ as their personal Savior.

We encourage them to start income-generating programs, like small businesses. We support them economically, socially, and spiritually. We introduce them to the digital world by assisting them in networking with organizations that can assist them through the Internet. Through the computer, they can obtain the skills necessary to help them make money.

This ministry conducts seminars to lift them from poverty, joblessness, hopelessness, drug abuse, fornication, and HIV/AIDS transmission. We are holding regular counseling sessions on entrepreneurial ventures and social problems affecting the youth.

We also have several community-based projects in towns, villages, and inner cities for AIDS orphans and disowned children, as well as widow feeding programs in the slums, vocational training centers for underprivileged youths, and rehabilitation centers for drug addicts.

I am doing hard work outside of my comfort zone. I'm helping needy people and leaving them better than I had found them. God is overcoming every hindrance and obstacle in my ministry. He has given me the qualities I need to fulfill His will in my life and ministry.

I have learned that there are eternal benefits of enduring hard times until the vision is fulfilled. I know how to comfort the brokenhearted and those who are in afflictions. When I show people I understand their problems, they respect me and pay attention because I was born and brought up in an impoverished and miserable family.

Today I have experience in helping the hopeless. This is the greatest asset in my ministry. I like encouraging hurt people as I tell them to trust in God and lean on Him so He can help them to solve their problems. I have encouraged orphans, widows, underprivileged youth, disowned children, vulnerable children, and the hurting. I have encouraged those who are going through hard times, like the loss of a job, a painful marriage, the loss of a loved one, a state of poor health, or other problems in life. I like quoting the word of God, "Don't weep" (Luke 7:13).

I encourage hurting people to trust in God and discover what He can do for their lives. I tell them the story of my life before I found God's redeeming love. God is good to me. "He brought me up out of a horrible pit, out of the miry clay, and set my feet upon a rock" (Ps. 40:2).

I tell people to trust in God, lift their voices, and begin to praise Him for who He is and what He can do in their troubled lives. God is good, and He will meet you at the point of your need, no matter what you are going through.

I know that I will keep on focusing on my vision, even if it tarries. God will make it come to pass in His own time. I believe that no vision comes without pain. I'm prepared to bear everything through Christ, who strengthens me.

My vision is developing like a child from conception to fulfillment. The first step of my vision came with intimacy with God. The second step was like conception when I became pregnant with my vision. With the third step, my vision started developing slowly through a divine process. The fourth step is expanding or maturing in the womb. The fifth step was traveling in prayer and being in great pain while the vision was about to be born.

I had to stay in a birthing position and then push until my vision was born. There is no vision without pain. I am very much encouraged by the story of Prophet Elijah; he was hiding in a cave because he feared that Ahab, the king, was searching to kill him. It came to pass after many days in the cave, for the word of the Lord came to Elijah in the third year, saying, "Go present yourself to Ahab, and I will send rain upon the Earth. So, Elijah went to present himself to Ahab, as there was a severe famine in Samaria" (1 Kings 18:1–2).

When the word of God came to Elijah, he was pregnant with a miracle of rain in his spirit for the people of Samaria. The first thing to do was to prove to these stubborn people that God has sent him to perform a miracle of rain and end the severe famine. Elijah had to prove to King Ahab that God would answer with fire.

"Immediately, the fire of the LORD flashed down from Heaven and burned up the young bull, the wood, the stones, and the dust. It even licked up all the water in the trench!" Then Elijah commanded, 'Seize all the prophets of Baal. Don't let a single one escape!' So, the people seized them all, and Elijah took them down to the Kishon Valley and killed them there." Then Elijah said to Ahab, "Go get something to eat and drink, for I hear a mighty rainstorm coming!" (1 Kings 18:2, 38, 40–41).

Before my vision was fulfilled, I had to fight all the opposing forces. I had to win the battle and breakthrough. I had to penetrate, make away, subdue, put under, and put to an end by force the operations of opposition.

Even the prophet, Elijah, had to fight the opposing forces of false prophets of Baal before he could receive a breakthrough. When he killed the false prophets of Baal, he received the greatest miracle; there was an outpouring of rain in Samaria. God is faithful.

Note what Elijah did before he experienced the miracle. "He...put his face between his knees" (1 Kings 18:42). That's to say that he was travailing in prayer. Firstly, this means total submission to his LORD, and secondly, this is the birthing position. He was experiencing pain, and yet he pushed until the miracle was born.

Then Elijah said to his servant, "Go and look out toward the sea." The servant went and looked, then returned to Elijah and said, "I didn't see anything." Seven times Elijah told him to go and look. Finally, the seventh time, his servant told him, "I saw a little cloud about the size of a man's hand rising from the sea." Then Elijah shouted, "Hurry to Ahab and tell him, 'Climb into your chariot and go back home. If you don't hurry, the rain will stop you!'" (1 Kings 18:2, 38, 40–41).

The first thing to do if you are pregnant with a vision or a miracle is to look up to the goal, not the people. The Bible says, "Blessed is the man who trusts in the Lord. He will be like a tree planted by the water that sends out its roots by the stream" (Jer. 17:7–8). This type of tree has no worries even in the year of famine or drought, and as a result, it never fails to bear fruits.

Elijah kept getting the same negative report from his servant, yet he kept on believing what God had told him. He kept on believing until the seventh time when the same servant finally reported to him, "There is a cloud as small as a man's hand rising out of the sea" (2 Kings 18:43).

Elijah stood on the promises of God in His word. He was not influenced by those who did not share his vision or miracle. He knew the word of God never fails and that God is faithful.

You must position yourself to receive a miracle; you must increase your faith and your expectancy. You must put your face between your knees. That means staying in a birthing position and then pushing hard. Today I'm reminded that I must remain in a birthing position and push until my vision or miracle is born. Now I can sense a great outpouring of the Holy Spirit in the continent of Africa that will sweep nations, and there will be a mighty revival in Africa. I'm obeying my vision to the end. What about you? To all those who are hurting, let me encourage you, "Do not weep" (Luke 7:13).

In Jesus Christ, you will find salvation, deliverance, and healing for your life. In Him, you will find answers in your troubled life. Why do you trust Him for salvation, deliverance, and healing? Because you will discover God is faithful to all those who trust and believe in Him. Trust Him now, and your life will be changed forever.

Do you know that every success, every vision, and every miracle starts with somebody taking a small step or sowing a small seed? Everything big starts with something small. If you are not ready to start small, you cannot start at all.

God loves to use the simple things that we think are insignificant. He used a boy's lunch to feed a multitude. He wants to use your small money, vision, gift, ministry, or idea to bless many. "There is a cloud as small as a man's hand rising from the sea" (2 Kings 18:44).

Often, the change that impacts many starts with one man. Remember people like Mother Teresa and Billy Graham? They did great things for the glory of God. God is calling you today to do great things for His glory.

Let my actions speak; make me too brave not to love and be kind. Make me too understanding to ignore the hurting people that no one else cares about. Help me to hear their innermost cries and help me carry their burdens.

"My God! Help me to answer their cries! Let me love them unconditionally. Let me be their joy and hope. Let my actions speak." This is my prayer in my ministry to give hope to the hopeless. There is a common adage, "Actions speak louder than words." Let my actions speak! The Bible encourages me to share with and do well to others. "But do not forget to do well and to share, for with such sacrifices God is well pleased" (Heb. 13:16).

Africa is in my heart!

Chapter 8

SURVIVING BY FAITH

I thank the Lord for His wonderful gift of salvation. It has been more that forty years since I invited Him into my heart. He appeared to me in 1985 in a thrilling dream of hope. Since then, I have been preaching the gospel to the poor.

In the year 2000, I relocated to Nairobi and started a church ministry in Githurai 45 Estate. I was always busy in the streets ministering hope to the poor, drug addicts, prostitutes, widows, orphans, criminals, drunkards, and victims of HIV/AIDS.

I had experienced opposition, trials, and many temptations, but the living God encouraged my ministry. He gave me enough grace to help me cope with any threatening situation.

Often I was in the Githurai slums doing evangelism day after day. It was an extremely challenging experience for me to minister hope to those hopeless lives. The needs of those poor people were immense, and their conditions were more complicated than I had thought.

I meet face-to-face with many hopeless people who do not know Jesus or the meaning of salvation, yet some of those people actually live only a few meters from the church. On nearly every street you could find two or three churches. You could also hear preachers preaching through the loudspeakers in the open air on every street corner.

The challenges of the very hard life many people were living were slowly becoming very real to me. I was concerned. I started to preach the gospel with boldness as if there was no church in the area.

The question to me from God was, "Are you willing to go where needy people live?" God gave me a very effective strategy for reaching the city dwellers. The approach I used was very simple. That's to be concerned about the needs of the poor and share their burden.

I swallowed my pride and entered their homes and shared their pain with love. Men, women, and youth opened their hearts to me as I showed them practical love. My life was bound together with the poor as they opened their hearts for a true witness of the love of God and Jesus, who died for us all. I helped them, through practical love, to understand the meaning of salvation as I focused on what God was doing in their midst. I was born and brought up in a rural area. However, I was changing from a rural preacher to an urban preacher.

The ministry in the city is very expensive because it costs a lot of money to organize a crusade or an open-air meeting. It costs money to do anything for God in the city.

People in the city are very busy trying to make ends meet. So, they will have been too busy to be involved in the ministry. They would leave their homes very early in the morning to go to work in the city center, and in the evenings come home very tired.

Many people migrate from rural areas into the city in search of jobs, and they find themselves landing in the slums. The city council administrators are unable to cope with the rapidly growing population of the poor in the slums.

Another major cause of poverty is corruption. This causes the little wealth and resources we have to not be distributed fairly. Land grabbing and greed can cause poverty.

Poverty in the city leads to crimes and substance abuse. Other effects of poverty are prostitution and AIDS pandemics. Another cause of poverty is the difficulty in finding employment. Many youths turn to crime to survive. Poverty leads to moral decay.

The Bible encourages me to minister hope to widows, orphans, refugees, and strangers (Gen. 18:1–5).

I am called to hear the cry of the poor and the needy. I am to be sensitive to their needs and their plight. God gave me a special concern for the poor in the city to save them from the hands of the devil and to give them hope.

The Bible says that Jesus was rich, but He made Himself poor so that He could meet the needs of the poor. The poor needed inward renewal and transformation. That's why I am using all available resources and moral persuasion in my endeavor to help them.

I have a platform to speak for the poor. My ministry to the poor is holistic for their physical, emotional, spiritual, and psychological needs.

The poor and the needy want the gospel of hope. They had been wanting to repent and to receive Christ. That's why I am busy in the streets preaching the gospel. Their needs moved me, and I was ready to provide food, shelter, and clothing to the homeless.

The church must act by showing practical love to the needy and the poor. This could be made possible by improving the prospects of their income generation programs; help them to start good and affordable small-scale businesses.

You can help them start vocational training programs and give them small loans to start their businesses with. This can help the hopeless youth break the cycle of poverty and joblessness.

Whenever I saw the street boys, I asked them how they could be helped to come out of their mess. I planned to make a feeding center, and I asked all church members to be involved with it.

Our ministry is very active in supporting development programs for the poor. We are very willing to network with other social welfare groups, NGOs, and other organizations, and we're always ready to learn from others.

If the church is to address these issues, we need to use all of our resources to reach the poor. I encourage every Christian to love, care for, and help the poor. Let us be like the famous mother, Teresa of Calcutta, who devoted her whole life to help the poor in India.

Let's get involved, and God will open doors for us. Let's volunteer to help the poor. It is only as we live like Jesus that we shall be able to impact the poor with the gospel of Christ. Thousands of poor people are living in challenging conditions in the slums and ghettos. They are asking, "Is there hope for us?"

City dwellers know my church as the temple of praise and worship. Every Sunday, we have received new members. We have the compassion to reach the unloved people. People who have lost hope for survival. Hopeless people who are desperately seeking answers in their lives.

We bring change to the lives of the poor and the hopeless. We are seeking willing leaders who will catch our vision of giving hope to the hopeless. Thousands of people are suffering, and they need somebody to encourage them. Remember that a word of hope or encouragement, a smile, or a helping hand can do good to the suffering.

We are aggressively addressing the issues affecting the poor. We are also outside the walls of the church teaching sound morals and biblical values. We encourage people by reading the word of God.

"I have told you all this so that you may have peace in me. Here on Earth, you will have many trials and sorrows. But take heart, because I have overcome the world" (John 16:33).

The word of God encourages me to press on with reaching the unreached and giving hope to the hopeless. Everywhere we look, we see signs of moral decay. Jesus is our only hope in this hurting world. The Bible says, "Do not let your hearts be troubled; trust in God, trust also in me" (John 14:1).

I understand if you are struggling with pain. Take all of your burdens, your problems, and your sins to the one who can save you and give you rest. Jesus is calling you, "Come to me all you who labor and are heavy laden, and I will give you rest" (Matt. 11:28). Stop struggling. Jesus wants to give you rest.

Jesus is willing to give you hope. He gave hope to a ruler in the synagogue. The desperate ruler was named Jairus. His daughter had died, but when the man cried to Jesus for help, Jesus encouraged him by telling him, "Fear not, only believe" (Luke 8:50). As a result of Jarius's belief, Jesus raised his daughter to life again. Jesus loves you, and He cares for every need in your life.

Whether you like it or not, you will get your share of troubles, but no matter how difficult your problem is, Jesus can calm every storm in your life. He will simply speak the word, "peace, be still," and you will find rest in your soul. Jesus has all the resources to save, heal, deliver, restore, renew, forgive, guide, comfort, encourage, strengthen, provide, and open doors for you.

The hope I have in Jesus Christ today is not wishful thinking, but rather it is the confident expectation that He is going to do what He says in His word. I live by faith in Him, and I possess all the promises in His word. Jesus is my only hope in life. "You are my refuge and my shield. I have put my hope in your word" (Ps. 119:114).

I have taken the word of God into my heart and trusted Him to fulfill His promises. I am confident that He will fulfill His word. I depend on Him whenever I need comfort, encouragement, guidance, or provision. I know that my redeemer lives in my heart.

I preach a holistic gospel, body soul and spirit. My ministry is very active in fighting HIV/AIDS. I am targeting youth in schools and colleges because they are active sexually and therefore very vulnerable. I am also helping the youth in slums on how to overcome youthful lust, fornication, and masturbation, as well as how to stop their other risky behaviors.

My aim is to sensitize the youth on their rights and teach them how to avoid premarital sex, drug abuse addiction, and prostitution. I am networking with other organizations that deal with substance abuse and HIV/AIDS issues.

It is amazing to note that many people across the world are very willing to make our vision a reality. With their help, we are making a difference in the cities. However, what we have done through the grace of God is but a drop in the ocean. More lost souls and needy people need to be reached before it is too late.

Jesus cares for us. He has a new path for our life. "Remember not the former things, nor consider the things of old. Behold, I am doing a new thing; now it springs forth. Do you not perceive it? I will make a way in the wilderness and rivers in the deserts" (Isa. 43:18–19).

God has a wonderful plan for your life. Obey His voice. Will you? He is asking you, "Behold, I am the Lord, the God of all flesh. Is there anything too hard for me?" (Jer. 32:27). Let me assure you that in Jesus Christ, we are more than conquerors. I am the messenger of hope who is serving as the herald of this new thing that God is doing in this world today. It is a word of hope to the hopeless and the poor.

I help the poor because I know that God blesses those who assist the poor. Another thing I know is that God can bless a poor man to become very rich. The Bible says, "Riches and honor are with me; enduring wealth and prosperity" (Ps. 18:18). Verse 20 says, "I walk in the way of righteousness; God can bless a poor man with wealth and fill his or her treasures." Also, "The poor man cried, and the Lord heard him and saved him out of all his troubles" (Ps. 34:6).

You can receive new hope for your life through the scriptures. God has good plans for your life. The Bible says, "The LORD makes some poor and others rich. He brings some down and lifts others up. He raises up the poor from the dust. He lifts the needy from the ash heap to make them sit with princes and inherit a seat of honor" (1 Sam. 2:7–8).

Never lose hope! God is about to raise you from the slums to the state house, from poverty to prosperity, because with God, nothing is impossible. Poverty is not a disability.

Suppose you have nothing to eat or anywhere to sleep. Jesus is giving you hope, saying, "Let not your heart be troubled; you believe in God, believe also in Me. In My Father's house are many mansions; if it were not so, I would have told you. I go to prepare a place for you. And if I go and prepare a place for you, I will come again and receive you to Myself; that where I am, and there you may be also" (John 14:1–3).

So, never lose hope. In Jesus Christ, there is hope for survival. "Now may the God of Hope fill you with all joy and peace in believing so that you may abound in hope by the power of the Holy Spirit" (Rom. 15:13). No one whose hope is in God is hopeless.

Chapter 9

THE HOPELESS

Our project to the needy is networked with other organizations, churches, and ministries around the world. God gave me a long-term vision, and I'm ever busy working for the implementation of the plan according to the vision in my life. I believe that God will help me to achieve my ultimate goal to glorify Him in this world.

The ministry is experiencing encouraging results. I will persistently and consistently remain on the track for which God has chosen me. My ministry is growing to be a large global organization to touch many hurting and needy souls. I am imparting hope to every needy person in society.

Apart from God's backing, the organization requires very committed volunteers and relief workers in order to make this project to the needy effective. I know God is preparing, equipping, and sending out our volunteers and relief workers. In our office in Nairobi, we are praying for this great project, as well as with this missionary enterprise, with a deep concern for the lost.

I am a messenger of hope, and that's why I go into the village, slums, and ghettos preaching the God of Hope to the hopeless. Thousands of hopeless and needy people are struggling to know Christ as their personal savior. Many of these people have lost hope, while others are searching for something to fill the craving in their souls. They are simply waiting for eternal doom.

God called me to go into places where people are struggling and suffering in sin. I have obeyed the voice of God in my life and don't want anything to shift my focus from my divine mandate to win souls for Christ. I am taking the universal cure to all those who are struggling with sin or terrible diseases. I have meant business in God's business. I am giving out living waters to these thirsty souls. The promise is, "I will pour water on him who is thirsty. I will pour floods upon the dry ground" (Isa. 44:3).

I am leading the hopeless and the needy to the Good Shepherd, Jesus Christ, so that they can find rest in their troubled lives. I'm gathering the lost into the loving hands of God. I am ministering hope to the brokenhearted, injured, wounded, weak, limping, and afflicted. I am comforting and encouraging the sorrowful and grieved.

I am always out there to find the one sheep, leaving behind me the ninety-nine in the fold. God has given me His shepherd's heart. I'm looking at the world through shepherd eyes. God cares for the hurts and wounds of the lost and needy. I'm taking them to their loving Father, who cares for all and is always there to help us and answer our cries. "The Lord is near to all who call on Him, to all who call on Him in truth" (Ps. 145:18).

God knows all of our problems and sees our hurts in a single glance. He explores the whole world and sees every dark corner in our hearts. Jesus is the Good Shepherd, and He loves His sheep. He is the one who watches over us carefully and protects us from even the slightest danger or harm in our lives. He searches our hearts and our lives until He finds us. His presence assures us that He is always with us. Like Jacob, let us all believe in the Good Shepherd in our lives. Let's worship Him. "God has been my shepherd all my life to this day" (Gen. 48:15).

Why would you want to live in fear, suffering, and pain? Come to the Good Shepherd now, and you will find the rest and the peace you have been searching for. The Bible says, "I am the Good Shepherd. The Good Shepherd gives his life for the sheep" (John 10:11).

There is suffering all over the world because people have rejected the Good Shepherd. Jesus is willing to help you overcome problems. People may leave or not be able to care for you, but Jesus will never leave you nor forsake you. He will deliver you from your sins and problems. He knows all about you. He knows your past, your present, and your future.

He knows the damage that the devil has caused in your life. He knows all the evil plans that the devil has for you. He knows all your limitations and would know all about a financial crisis that may be overwhelming you right now. He knows if your heart is broken, and He would know how to fix it.

Jesus is willing and ready to give you a new start in life. To provide you with new strength to go on. He will comfort and encourage you, for He knows the weight of your burdens. He is ready and willing to listen to your hurts and your cries. Why are you struggling alone? Call the Good Shepherd into your heart now, and you will see the difference. He is alive and will lead you into the green pastures beside the still waters.

I have given Him my life. It is my heart's desire to live in His wonderful love and presence. I pray like Moses, "Lord, show protection and proper nourishment." Jesus loves me, and He is preparing and equipping me for His ministry. I see Him touching the lost and the needy. He is concerned with their sorrows and their grief.

As a messenger of the gospel, I make sure that the word of God is shared with these hopeless souls. We are sharing the heavenly treasures with the lost in Africa. Could you please join us in bringing one or two souls into the caring hands of our Savior?

Many children are suffering from rejection from their parents. We have thousands of marriages break up in divorce. Young people are suffering from both physical and sexual abuse. Others are suffering from a lack of employment. Many husbands cannot fulfill parental responsibilities. Teenagers are suffering from a serious loss of morals and self-respect, developing a certain degree of distrust and disrespect for their parents. They lose hope and involve themselves in drug abuse, crime, prostitution, and alcoholism. These evils are rampant in our villages, slums, and ghettos.

Some people's hurts and wounds are quite severe. They desperately need careful counseling. Such hopeless lives are sometimes difficult to bring into the presence of the wonderful counselor, Jesus Christ. I ensure that the needy regain their wholesome sense of identity and value in their lives. I make sure that all their hurts and wounds are healed in Jesus's name. I introduce needy people to the wonderful counselor, Jesus.

I will minister to their needs without working for money or any material benefits. I'm willing to serve them in an honorary capacity in all ways. I am using every possible opportunity and talent to minister to those hurting souls. It is God who called me, and I will obey His voice and the vision of my ministry. I need devoted people with a willing heart to support me in this outreach.

My time is spent in preaching, teaching, counseling, and visiting the needy in their homes. I get involved with other people's needs without having the time to think about my own needs. Some of the people I visit are actually in the same situation that I used to be in before I was saved. I make sure that I give them hope for a better future. I have helped many people recover from depression, stress, and the economic and social problems they have been in. Let us volunteer to address these issues and help the hurting souls to survive.

Some of the people I have ministered to are amazed by the way God is using me to address their personal problems. Sometimes it is very encouraging to look straight into the eyes of the needy and declare, "Jesus knows what you are going through." I tell them Jesus cares. I let them know I also care for their needs because I was brought up in a very miserable life. I know the horror of living in the slums. I use some of my experiences in life to encourage and comfort the needy. I know the distress. Thank God that I'm now free from that miserable life.

My problem now is, "What can I do to meet the needs of the people who are vulnerable to suffering in this evil society?" Yes, I have answered their cry, but I do not have enough to meet their immediate needs. Whether you care to admit it or not, it's only Jesus Christ who is able to save, heal, and satisfy all those hurting souls. The question is, "What are YOU doing to help save those hurting souls before it is too late?"

These souls are searching for meaning in their lives. They are trapped in a timeless state of poverty, hopelessness, frustration, suffering, and pain. They do not know where to turn for help. They are forced to adopt a culture of doubt and despair in life. Every day they are going deeper and deeper into hell. Their souls are hurting. They ask, "Is there hope for us?"

There is hope, for we have the God of hope. To all those who are wallowing in sin and despair, there is hope for all those who are at the crossroad and do not know where to turn for help. For poor people, who have no savings and are living from hand to mouth, there is hope. Needy people need Jesus, and they urgently need the life-sustaining and unfailing love of God.

We are gently responding to the needs of those hurting souls. And we are not contented to stay within the church compound but rather we are always out there in the community, where the hurting souls are. We must go beyond the church compound. We must extend the love of God to the lost and the needy who would never come into a church. God's love demands our loving activities.

Try to imagine now these hurting souls who are living in the slums and the ghettos. Their pain is beyond words. If you were to just visit them once in their homes, you would instantly feel their powerful emotions. May the Lord speak to you and touch you to do something to meet other people's needs. Just volunteer to encourage and comfort these hurting souls. They are trapped in a very terrible situation.

Remember. The hurting people could be asking, "Why me, Lord?" Even David, the king, cried to God, "I cry aloud to the Lord— I pour out my complaint before Him; before Him I tell my troubles" (Ps. 42:1–2). When the king was in distress, he prayed, "Be merciful to me, O Lord, for I am in distress, my soul and my body with grief. But I trust in you, O Lord; I say you are my God. My times are in your hands" (Ps. 31:9-15).

We are healing troubled souls by trying to establish the cause of their problems. It's noteworthy that even some Christians in this area suffer in the same ways. I am very sensitive when addressing such issues in their lives. The best encouragement is to tell the needy, "I know what you are going through."

Healing comes when you are open to listening to their problems. Many are helped by simply listening to their problems. Are you experiencing any problems in your life? Just be open to talking to us. Jesus is inviting you to bring your burden, and He will give you rest. "Take my yoke upon you and learn from me, for I am gentle and humble in heart, and you will find rest for your souls" (Matt. 11:28–29).

Jesus is willing to save you and to heal your broken heart. The Bible says, "The Lord is close to the brokenhearted and saves those who are crushed in spirit" (Ps. 34:18).

Let me remind you that whatever situation or circumstance you could be in now, the Lord is willing to save you, heal you, and deliver you from it now. Jesus is alive, and He has promised in His word that, "I will never leave you: and I will never forsake you" (Heb. 13:5).

Jesus loves you. Why don't you believe that He is speaking to you? There is hope for you. It is my prayer that the God of hope will meet your every need now. I would encourage you that it's appropriate to thank God for the many blessings we have received in the ministry. How do we do that, you may ask? Do we send him a card? No. We can simply lift up our eyes heavenward and say, "Thank you, Lord!"

We are sure about His wonderful leading through the Holy Spirit. I would ask you that even if you are a person who is not saved or a rich businessman. It's good to be thankful to God for your life and what you have in it. Remember. Gratitude is an emotion that should come from within you. Some people are sick in hospitals. Some are in prisons. Others are in very painful situations in their lives.

Even if your condition is not exactly as you would like it to be, it is better to lift up your eyes and begin to thank the Lord. "May the God of Hope fill you with all joy and peace as you trust in Him, so that you may overflow with hope by the power of the Holy

Spirit" (Rom. 15:13). We have a good God; a God for the hopeless. And I am a messenger of hope who preaches hope to the hopeless.

Chapter 10

GNAWING PAIN OF FAMINE

I was born in the outskirts of Nakuru city and I was raised in Kiambogo settlements farm by poverty stricken parents. We endured suffering from famine because of climate change. I hustled up food, jobs and burnt charcoal to feed my siblings. "Will the world leaders give us solutions to the climate change crisis?" Everybody is wondering.

After my salvation, I joined the village church. I started as an evangelist, although villages thought that I could not succeed, but eventually, I became a Pastor and later became a Bishop of Gospel Messengers Church, Kenya. I'm a patron of a community based organization in my location. Knowing what it meant to be hungry and malnourished, I volunteered to be a messenger of hope to millions of Kenyan families who were at a high risk of food security and malnourished.

Never Lose Hope is a true story of how God blessed me from a hustler to a presiding Bishop. In this book I'm encouraging the hopeless, the hurting and the needy. We are helping them to overcome the fear of the unknown. I help them to navigate through life by trusting in God, the creator of all things. God who is able to satisfy all people in the world physically and spiritually.

His power can save all from the climate change crisis and from the gnawing pain of famine which is caused by climate change. Thank God I was transformed from a hustler to a Bishop. With God everything is possible. God gave me a vision of reaching the unreached and giving hope for the hopeless. I also ministered to the hungry.

The hungry are the ones without anything to eat. We have millions who are hungry in Africa. We have millions of people living without shelter, clothing, clean water, or medical care. One of the major causes of famine is a change of climate in our continent. Another cause of famine is our high population growth rates. We have examples of famine in countries like Sudan, Somalia, and Ethiopia.

This is made worse by compaction by leaders who do not equitably distribute the wealth or the little food that we do have in our nations. This causes very high food prices, which in turn cause more hunger for those who cannot afford to buy their food. This brings about family stress as well as dehumanizing and demoralizing circumstances. Many families are living in loneliness and mental anguish.

Many have lost hope for survival. They have lost hope for a better future. This makes the youth, who are living in the slum areas, involve themselves with crimes to survive. Hunger has led many nations into general moral decay.

That is why I am very sensitive to the plight of the hungry. God has given me a special gift to minister hope to the hungry. Jesus said, "I was hungry, and you gave me something to eat" (Matt. 25:35).

I have a spiritual mandate to address the problem of the hungry. The church must be willing to do what Jesus did in the ministry. That's why I am very willing to share my resources with the hungry. I am ready to preach a holistic gospel to meet the physical, spiritual, emotional, and psychological needs of the hungry. The gospel must address the social needs of the hungry to be effective.

Let us feed the hungry and the homeless. We are improving the prospects of their income-generating programs, and we can assist in starting vocational training and the processing of small loans. As a Christian ministry, we must try our best to answer the cry of the hungry. Let us encourage our members in the churches to help the hungry in their neighborhoods, as the Bible says.

If you are a Christian, I can challenge you to be like Mother Theresa of Calcutta, India, who used to answer the cry of the hungry, the poor, and the needy. So, let us give to the hungry with a Christian heart. Let us remove the great gap in Africa between those who have and those who do not have. Let every member from high-class, middle-class, or low-class churches join together in helping the hungry.

Let us unite and break the walls that are separating these three groups in the churches as we help the hungry together. God is asking us now, "Whom shall I send, and who will go for Us? Then I said, Here I am! Send me" (Isa. 6:8).

A few months ago, the newspaper headlines carried full pages of shocking stories of the looming food crisis in Kenya. Stories were told of the escalating food prices and the problems that people are experiencing to access food.

For many years our beloved country used to be the promised land with a lot of food, milk, and honey. But today, millions of people in Kenya are being haunted by hunger, poverty, and starvation. We are terribly hit by famine.

Many families in some parts of Kenya are going to bed without a meal. I empathize with the many school children who endure hardships every day. It is my hope that the government will revive the school-feeding program. People in Kenya are dying of hunger because they cannot afford the high prices of the little food that is available. Many essential commodities have gone up in price, and this has been making life unbearable for the poor and the needy.

Maize beans, cabbage, potatoes, rice, sugar, tomatoes, and meat are among the commodities that are going up in price daily. Retail prices have shot up, and traders are selling food products at exorbitant prices. The traders at the open-air markets have increased the prices because of the shortage of supplies of the essential commodities.

The citizens of Kenya are crying to the government to correct this inflation. I hope that the government will focus on school children and provide them with at least two meals a day: one in school and one at home. We are trying hard as a ministry to fight the large-scale starvation and other social turmoil in society.

The Food and Agriculture Organization of the United Nations (FAO) has warned that pregnant mothers, children, and the elderly are particularly at risk from these food shortages.

The answers to these problems lie in boosting local food production. We must give the farmers quality seeds and fertilizers. This will allow the farmers to increase food production, and food production will make food prices go down. We are hoping for the best for the farmers in Kenya.

The Bible encourages us by saying, "Who shall separate us from the love of Christ? Shall tribulation or distress, persecution or famine, or nakedness or peril or sword?" (Rom. 8:36).

You can ask yourself, "What is famine?" Have you ever asked yourself this question? I know the gnawing pains of hunger as I can say that I have been one of the victims of it. I know what it is all about. I know there are those who are hungry right now.

Other people are malnourished. People who are malnourished do not have hunger pains all the time, but they have lived on a substandard diet for so long, they have adjusted to being chronically undernourished. They don't have the average amount of energy. They don't think very clearly. Sometimes they are tormented by diseases.

In Africa, we have been experiencing different images of famine over the decades. Some of you may remember the recent disturbing pictures of famine victims in various parts of Africa. You could see millions of starving people, including small children.

The image of famine is changing over the years, but the brutal fact is that even now as I write, millions of people do not have enough food to eat. Many of them are starving at this very moment. What can such people do? Let us ask all those people with the resources to offer out of their abundance and feed those in grave need of food. This must be done to alleviate starvation, and it must be done quickly. Let us attack the root causes of famine and malnutrition.

The root cause of starvation in some nations of Africa is the lack of rain. People need food and water during this time of drought in their land. That's where you find millions of refugees trying to find food. People are struggling to find the basic necessities of survival.

All of the issues that can lead to hunger must be addressed. Education on better farming methods is urgently needed in rural areas. Farmers must be taught how to be self-sufficient and how to feed others. It's one thing to buy a hungry man a lunch, but it's a far different thing to educate that person on how to provide food for himself.

Let's focus on how to support farmers in rural areas. Let us help them to help themselves, and thereby help others in need. Let us help all those who are desperately hungry.

Jesus came into the world to bring light to those who are starving. It is a horrible thought that millions of the world's people are in misery because they do not have enough food.

Through our combined efforts, we can work to get enough food to feed millions in Africa. The problem is that we lack the knowledge, and that we also lack responsibility. And to compound the problem, we also have civil conflicts that are leaving millions of people destitute and homeless.

Our ministry is helping those in need. We are providing long-term solutions to the hunger problem by teaching rural folk how to properly plant and care for their crops. We have a will to give them moral support.

We must keep our faith. That compels us to leave the comfort of our lives and go out to the places where the hungry are. Many of our friends are leaving their comfortable homes and good jobs to help people who are in need. We have been working with local churches to help meet the needs of the hopeless. We need people with a sacrificial spirit in their lives to come alongside us in this work.

We need people of great faith to help the needy. We don't only think of food for the stomach, but also food for eternal life. The greatest responses to the needs of the hungry are carried out in the name of Jesus Christ. Along with helping farmers to farm more effectively, we tell them about Christ.

Remember. In this life, circumstances change. Times change. The day may come when you will be in desperate need. It could happen to you, so depend on God and remember the ones in need.

Although we must work hard to provide for our families, we must be willing to help others, too. I know some people who share the little they have with others in need. That is the true spirit of God's unfailing love.

Remember that all those who do not have something to eat are our brothers and sisters. Don't ever forget the hungry. Don't ever assume that you could never be in such a situation at some point in your life as well. You could be saying today that you have a lot of food in your store and don't need any help from anyone. Don't ever fool yourself in that way. A disaster could be coming your way one day, and you could be asking for help.

Don't ever think that you are different from all those who are starving. Remember the Lord's Prayer, "Give us today our daily bread." A lot of adjustment is required in your life before you'll have a heart for the needy. You must learn the basic elements of the needy. You must have a heart full of generosity.

Thank God for all the blessings that He has given you. In Kenya, we are thanking God for the abundant blessings in this part of Africa. We have encouragement for our harvests. We have been receiving rain, and sometimes the harvests are extremely good.

Also, thousands of people are employed, and those who are employed have received an increase in their salaries. The economy is experiencing an upward turn, and we have no reason to wonder about the future of our people. We are very grateful to God, who has helped Kenya to improve in many areas in general.

We are comparing our lives with those in other parts of Africa, and we see that some other nations are plagued by crop failures and others are riddled by political strife. That's why we have a lot to be thankful for in our country.

Take a close look at our continent. Millions of people are dying of hunger. That is why we should always pray the Lord's Prayer. Remember. It was Jesus who fed the 5,000 people when He said, "You give them something to eat" (Mark 6:37).

It will take your effort and commitment to volunteer to work with us. Together, we shall make great strides. I do believe that every project targeted will be achieved. We need many volunteers from different parts of the world. Our projects will be continually proven and redefined to suit our supporters. We are going to offer a totally personalized advisory service to our volunteers. This will cover all of our programs in the projects.

We are asking our volunteers to concentrate on one project first. Why not write to us and enjoy your work as a volunteer, or give us your support? If you volunteer, God will give you a burden to serve others, and we shall be praying for you. I will make a declaration of a breakthrough and victory in your life. The Bible says, "Thou shall also decree a thing, and it shall be established unto thee" (Job 22:28).

As you follow God in your life, you will have everything to gain and nothing to lose. I am praying for you. You will prosper, and you will succeed in your life. We have testimonies all over the world from those partners and volunteers who have prospered. We always hope to see the hopeless receiving Jesus Christ as their personal savior. May God help you support us to carry on with our dream of giving hope to the hopeless in Africa. Together, let us echo the cry, "Africa belongs to Jesus!"

What we have done now is but a drop in the ocean. More souls need you in order to be reached before it is too late. Could you please uphold Africa in your prayers? Although peace is indeed very rare in our hate-filled Africa, we are declaring peace in this troubled continent in Jesus's name. My prayer is, "Lord, turn Africa with your power and give us peace." God's love brings peace.

I can hear the voice of Jesus speaking to all the storms in Africa, saying, "Peace, be still." That's why I am not wavering in my actions. He who began a good work in our lives will see us through. We must be anchored in the Rock, the unshakable Rock, and the solid foundation. In Jesus, we shall overcome all the storms in Africa.

Let us, therefore, lift our eyes up to where our help comes from. Our help comes from the Lord. Blessed is the man who puts his trust in the Lord because in times of the storms and evil, he will find hope in God. "May the God of Hope fill you with all joy and peace in believing so that by the power of the Holy Spirit, you may abound in hope" (Rom. 15:13).

I preach hope. Is your situation beyond hope? Is your hope dead? With Jesus, you can rise above your storm. Never lose hope. Jesus is Alive. The whole world is warned about overpopulation. Experts predict that unless dramatic action is taken very gently to curb the growing population, the world will be a mess.

Today, the world's population has already risen to over six billion people, and it is growing at a very rapid rate. That's to say that we are not able to feed this increased population.

In Africa, millions of people go hungry and undernourished. As the population increases, the demand for food increases, but the supply of food decreases. Therefore, we experience rising food prices rising daily.

Jesus said that famines would be one of the signs of the end of the world. The Book of Revelation in the Bible tells us that the time is coming when a measure of wheat will be sold for a day's wage.

That's why I am telling you about this catastrophe that is affecting us in Africa. Are you putting your hope on money, or silver and gold? The Bible says, "Go to now, you rich men. Weep and howl for your miseries that shall come upon you. ...Your gold and silver is cankered" (James 5:1,3).

Millions of people are dying of hunger. Jesus is our only hope! It is Jesus alone who can save you from the gnawing pain of famine. Never lose hope. Call Jesus now. He is alive. In several places in Kenya, we have been experiencing famine, and we have to look to Jesus for survival. We are experiencing turbulent and difficult times. Along with famine, we have been experiencing continued violent conflicts and a significant shaking in the world of finances.

Our hope is not in this evil and crooked world. It is within Christ. We are putting our hope in Christ and in the world to come. God is on the throne, and nothing happens unless He allows it to happen. Everything is working with an internal purpose. All things work together for good.

Things that happen may not be good in themselves, but God will ultimately work them for good. God's grace is sufficient in our lives, and nothing can separate us from the love of God in Jesus Christ. "For I am persuaded that neither death nor life, nor angels, nor principality, nor powers, nor things present, nor things to come, nor height, nor depth, nor any created thing, shall be able to separate us from the love of God, which is in Christ Jesus, our Lord" (Rom. 8:38–39).

Our ministry consists of outreaches in the famine-hit areas. We share food and simple gospel messages with the victims. We have met with hungry mothers carrying wailing infants for many kilometers to get a small package containing about five kilos of maize flour. We are also giving them the bread of life that gives eternal life. We are addressing the gnawing pain of famine in Africa. Please join us in the fight against hunger.

Never Lose Hope!

MANY PEOPLE IN AFRICA are suffering without food as a result of famine and floods. Millions of people are starving; good and innocent people who have been living with good-paying farms find themselves fleeing elsewhere to find food and other basic necessities of survival.

Because we are messengers of God, we have the compassion to help our brothers and sisters who have nothing to eat. Our humanitarian project has recently developed an ambitious plan to help, aimed at transforming many lives. We are using modern, efficient, and effective ways to reach out in love.

We are responsible for helping the hungry people to have their needs met. The specter of famine that leads to death is worrisome, and we should not spare our resources to combat it. We have daily reports filtering into our offices from Christian workers who tell us how people are starving in different parts of Africa due to crop failures. For this reason, people find themselves in precarious situations. These severe food shortages have resulted in death and misery for many people in Africa.

We are crying out to generous people around the world to give us food donations to help these starving people. Famine often comes suddenly, and the tragedy is that we are unable to take measures to prevent it because of a lack of funds.

Remember. We are living in this world in uncertainty because seasons change, situations change, conditions change, governments change, and nations change. The weather changes, but Jesus is the same yesterday, today, and forever (Heb.13:8).

We are to revisit the whole question of food donations and how to set out clear strategies to avoid scarcity in the future. Weather patterns are beyond man's control, but we are to help the hopeless farmers with farming resources such as seeds and fertilizers to plant when the weather is favorable to eliminate cases of famine.

We are asking our brothers and sisters in the world who can spare funds to help overcome this famine crisis. It is good to help the starving by providing them with food and then educating them on how to overcome such situations in the future.

Join us in this life-changing ministry. Our ministry evangelism must address all aspects of a human being. We are called to share our daily bread with the starving and to cover the naked. The Bible says, "Then shall your light break forth like the dawn, and your healing shall spring up speedily; your righteousness shall go before you, and the glory of the Lord shall be your rear guard. Then you shall call, and the Lord will answer. He will say, 'Here I am'" (Isa. 58:7–9).

In my life, I have known what it means to be hungry and malnourished. Recently we have been looking at the disturbing pictures of people starving in Ethiopia, Sudan, Somalia, and other parts of Africa. We are concerned with helping the starving because we know that the Lord has promised special blessings to all those who minister to the hungry. Jesus is making a wonderful way on our continent. In our ministry, we are trying to make a difference in this hurting world. God is changing African society, regardless of the present economic conditions.

Africa does not just need more religion when millions of people are suffering without somebody to help. We do not need more mega-church buildings to be built while the people's basic needs are being ignored by our religious leaders. We are called to portray Jesus Christ in our lives in all ways, just like the disciples.

When the disciples helped others, the Church increased in number, and the gospel was easily marketed.

The word of God says, "If you draw out your soul to the hungry and satisfy the afflicted soul, then your light will rise in drought and make fat your bones. You shall be like a watered garden, and like a spring of water whose waters fail not" (Isa. 58:10–11).

We are willing to help the starving in whatever capacity we might be able to. We have created a channel through this project to share our resources with the hungry. Never Lose Hope.

About Us

Gospel Messengers Church is a nonprofit dedicated to transforming lives in Kenya's most marginalized communities. Committed to eradicating female genital mutilation (FGM), poverty, and illiteracy, the organization builds schools, provides clean water through boreholes, and empowers communities through education and sustainable development.

By addressing social injustices and uplifting vulnerable populations, Gospel Messengers Church fosters hope and opportunity for the less fortunate.

You can Donate via M-Pesa Pay Bill no: 880100 a/c: 5146870014.

You can also use PayPal email: messengergospel13@gmail.com

THESE ARE OUR BANK DETAILS FOR INTERNATIONAL MONEY TRANSFERS.

Bank Name	NCBA BANK KENYA PLC
Branch Name	NAKURU
Branch Code	000 (for any branch)
Bank Full Address	P.O. BOX 44599–00100, NAIROBI – KENYA
Bank Account Name	GOSPEL MESSENGER CHURCH
Bank Code	07
Bank Account Number	5146870014
SWIFT /BIC Code	CBAFKENX

Also by Peter N Muya

Kill Me Not
Love Without Lust
Do Not Weep
Death From Illicit Brew
Hope For Survival
I Shall Not Die
Never Lose Hope

Watch for more at https://www.gospelmessengerschurch.com.